Denis A. Quinn

Stenotypy

Or, Shorthand by the typewriter

Denis A. Quinn

Stenotypy
Or, Shorthand by the typewriter

ISBN/EAN: 9783337385965

Printed in Europe, USA, Canada, Australia, Japan

Cover: Foto ©Paul-Georg Meister /pixelio.de

More available books at **www.hansebooks.com**

Stenotypy:

OR SHORTHAND BY THE TYPEWRITER.

WHEREBY 120 WORDS PER MINUTE CAN BE STRUCK OFF
BY AN *ORDINARY* AND 300 WORDS PER MINUTE
BY AN *EXPERT* TYPEWRITER.

— — -

A SYSTEM, WHICH FROM ITS NUMEROUS DECIDED ADVANTAGES
OVER ALL KNOWN TREATISES ON PHONO AND STENOGRAPHY,
WILL ENTIRELY DISPENSE WITH THE USE OF THESE SYSTEMS
IN THE TELEGRAPH OFFICE AND COUNTING ROOM WHERE
TYPEWRITING MACHINES HAVE BEEN IN USE. IT IS ESPECIALLY
INVALUABLE FOR THE PRINTING TELEGRAPH.

— — -

The principles of the system can be learned in a few hours, and sufficient speed acquired in
the time required to manipulate with speed an ordinary typewriting machine.
The system can be adopted to any first-class typewriting machine.

SECOND IMPROVED EDITION.

BY REV. D. A. QUINN.

PROVIDENCE, R. I.: THE CONTINENTAL PRINTING CO.,
DYER AND PINE STREETS.
1895.

PREFACE.

THE AUTHOR

* does not by the title page mean to insinuate that Stenotypy will supersede Phonography in all its adaptations. On the contrary, he wishes to state that the system can be used only in connection with typewriting machines.

While the pen and pencil are more portable, it will be seen at once that Phonography is available in various departments where it would be inconvenient or impossible to use machines.

However, the Author makes bold to assert that wherever a typewriter is available, Stenotypy has decided advantages over all other shorthand systems. Whenever a typewriter shall be invented that can easily be carried in the pocket (we hope to see it soon in the market), indeed, phono and stenography will be universally discarded as obsolete and unworthy of a progressive age.

A few of the advantages of Stenotypy are noted on the next two pages.

---

*Lest anyone should consider this system constructed on a superficial basis, the Author begs to state that being thoroughly acquainted, for several years, with Pitman's, Munson's, Graham's, and Odell's systems of phono and stenography, he has thoroughly investigated the difficulties and advantages of Stenotypy, and is pleased to state that if the few rules given in the following treatise are strictly observed, there will be no confusion of words or sentences, while the reading of the abbreviated words will be a pleasure rather than an onerous task.

In cases where all the word signs of the alphabet are not attached to any particular machine, the operator must use the usual phonetic mode of spelling.

Advantages

OF STENOTYPY.

1. The system can be learned in a few hours, and requires no more practice than is generally devoted to acquire speed in ordinary type-writing.

2. Stenotypy is exceedingly more legible than any system of phonography or shorthand. In Pitman's, Graham's, Barnes', Pernin's, and all other less popular systems, one sign is made to represent *two*, and sometimes *three* letters. For instance : To write the words catholic, character, queen, king, only one sign for the initial letter of each of these letters is phonographically given. X and Q are left out in all phonographic systems. Every reporter knows how difficult it is to designate by heavy and light strokes, or half or double length st okes, P, T; F, V; CH, J; K, G; S, Z, &c. In Stenotypy all the letters of the Alphabet (soft and hard, long or short), may be used, thereby rendering the reading less difficult. It is very easy for a shorthand writer to dash off eighty or 100 words per minute ; but it often requires *years* of practice to read what has been so quickly written. Stenotypy is especially adapted for facile reading, besides being adapted to a speed far greater than phonography could ever attain.

3. It must be remembered that Stenotypy has all the advantages of phonography, besides it expresses words and sounds by their proper letters, just as they are printed in a book or newspaper. Ksrss ; estion, of Pitman style, are not as legible as the abbreviated form of Stenotypy : xrcs ; qstion, meaning exercise. question. In all systems of shorthand the exact positions of signs *above, upon* and *below* the line ; also, *perpendicular* and *horizontal* positions, and *half* and *double length* lines must be carefully expressed lest the reading should be rendered impossible. Oftentimes life and property have been jeopardized by the mistaking of a *half* for a *full* or a *double stroke* ; or a sign *on* for a sign *above* or *below* the line. Stenotypy can have no letter out of position ; a single tap of the key defines the character of each letter.

4. Stenotypy dispenses with Pitman's awkward use of *heavy* and *light* strokes and triple positions, as also Pernin's small, large and larger circles and loops for vowels,

5

and lines and *divisions* of lines for consonants. As a shorthand writer of thirty years experience, the Author found more difficulty in finding out the *position* and *length* of lines or curves than to guess the words in their non-vowel form. In rapid writing it is almost impossible to guide a pen or pencil so that it will distinctly mark *vertical, oblique* and *horizontal* half or full lines or curves. Yet, the *reading*, as every reporter knows, depends on the *size* and *position*. With the typewriter, there is no such difficulty. In most cases it is easier to read exercises in Stenotypy than sentences spelled in their full or othographic entirety. Stenotypy is a boon to all aspiring David Copperfields.

5. While the phonographic manuscript can be read only by the writer or reporter himself, Stenotypy, being based on the letters of the Alphabet (firmly attached to the machine,) can be read at any time by anyone who understands the language.

6. Whilst scarcely one out of a hundred ever acquires sufficient speed in phonography, the practice of Stenotypy is a pleasant exercise, easily learned, and great speed can be acquired by anyone of ordinary ability.

7. Frequently, the most learned persons are sorry penmen. In Stenotypy nervous and awkward persons are often the fastest typewriters. It may, at once, be understood that anyone who is expert at the typewriter, will have no difficulty whatever in becoming a speedy Stenotypist.

8. Stenotypy dispenses with the use of text and exercise books, and saves the time (averaging from six to twelve months) necessary to acquire proficiency in shorthand, besides the expenses of a teacher.

9. As no pen wielded by a human hand can compete in speed with an ordinary typewriter, for the same reason can no reporter or penman write as fast as a Stenotypist. Stenotypy is simply shorthand operated by a typewriter.

STENOTYPY AND THE PRINTING TELEGRAPH.

10. Of the numerous departments in which stenotypy can be utilized, perhaps, telegraphy is the most important. At present telegraph operators have adopted an abbreviated code for transmitting words. It is founded on phonetics, but is not governed by any rule. An illustration will best describe it. An operator in Washington, transmitting a special dispatch to an operator in New York, clicks off the following :—

Desines r bg prepard at t buro o eng & ptg for new issue o 5 dol slvr ctfs t drwgs hvg bn furnished by Blashfleld. On t face o these notes wl b sh intricate traceries & envgs as to deter t most drg fm even atmptg to counterfeit em, t pvallg tone bg slvr gra.

The expert typewriter " receiver " turns out this translation of the jargon.

Designs are being prepared at the Bureau of Engraving and Printing for a new issue of $5 silver certificates. The drawings having been furnished by Blashfleld. On the face of these notes will be such intricate traceries and engravings as to deter the most daring from even attempting to counterfeit them, the prevailing tone being a silver gray.

In the foregoing abbreviated form there are 200 letters and 52 word spacings, while in the translation there are 280 letters and 52 word spaces ; so that 80 letters are saved by the telegraph code. Now, in writing the above extract according to the rules of Stenotypy, we find that instead of 80, we save 130 letters and 43 space taps, or a net saving of 173 taps on the transmitter, whilst the reading is immensely facilitated. Every character of Stenotypy is founded on phonetic principles. Prefixes, affixes and word characters are clearly represented, and on account of the frequency of *capital* letters, the attention of the eye is more easily arrested. In order to fully comprehend the principles of Stenotypy, and thoroughly understand the key that unravels all its apparent difficulties, only the *Alphabet*, or two pages of the booklet has to be memorized. The grammalogues, and arbitrary signs used are fewer than those used by Pittman, Graham, Pernin, &c.

The Author feels confident, that after two weeks' study, any ordinary student can read *all* the exercises in the present volume.

The following is the above telegraph message written according to Stenotypy :—

ds Ins Rb, ; prd T'bUrOFngr v, &prnt, 4&nUi)UF5$s l vr cr t fk 8s'drw, H, bn frn)dB B1) f ld. N'f9F(s n@sLBs$ ntrk8trs3s&ngr v, Z2dtr'ms t dAr, frmEvn tmp t, 2 2ft (m'; vl, tOmb, &s l vr grA.

Indeed, any one capable of judging of the merits of Stenotypy must admit that there is not in existence a more efficient, and at the same time a shorter and simpler treatise on shorthand than the present little volume.

ALPHABET AND KEY

TO STENOTYPY.

CAPITALS.	GRAMMALOGUES.	SUFFIXES
B	be, by, but.	
C	say, see, sea.	
D	day, die, do.	
F	if, of, off.	
G	God. go, age.	-age.
H	he, have, him.	
J	Jesus, jew.	·ness-ship.
K	can, no, know. (Kt can't.)	
L	Lord, all, will.	
M	may, me, my, am.	
N	in, on, under. (N- only.)	
P	up, upon, people.	
Q	queen. quack, quick.	-head-hood.
R	are, or, our, Mr. (Rss *Messrs* Rs ours.)	
S	she, shall, so.	
T	that, it, out.	
U	you, ye.	
V	very, every, over, ever.	
W	we, who, was, with. (W- wholly.)	
X	Christ. (Xn christian.)	·oxy.
Y	they, thee, thy, thou. (Y'n thine.)	
Z	as, is, us. (Ze use.)	
$	ch, dollar, each, church.	
(	th	
)	sh	

ALPHABET AND KEY

CONTINUED.

CAPITALS.	PREFIXES.	SUFFIXES.
2	contra, contri, contro, counter.	
3	enter, inter, intro, intru.	-try-ary-ory.
4	magna, magne, magni.	-fore-dom.
5	trans.	-ive-ife-ful.
6	accom, accum, accoun.	-ion-sion-self.
7	encom, incon, encoun, incog.	-able-ible-ment.
8	recom, recog.	-ate-ity-tude.
9	retra, retre, retri, retro.	-ace-acy-ice.
%	circum. (per cent.)	-ony-mony.
#	hypo, hyper. (number.)	-ember-gress.
/	after, afore.	-ake-ike-oke.
&	{ a, an, and, one. (&c. once, cm&7 commandment.)	-and.
'	(comma over the line) the.	
,	(comma on line)	-ing-s.
-	(dash)	-ly-less.
:	(colon)	-us-ous-ions.
@	at.	-ite-ote-ute.
"	com, con, cor.	
;	pri, pre, pro, pru.	
—		-ward-part.
ç	cent-s.	-ant-ent.
c	catholic, character.	(with space to right and left.)
d	doctor.	" " " " " "
n	nothwithstanding, nevertheless.	" " " " " "
o	circumstance, world.	" " " " "
p	particular, peculiar.	" " " "
x	extra, extraordinary.	" " " "

9

GRAMMALOGUES, PREFIXES, AFFIXES,
FIGURES, ETC.

Grammalogues may be used to form the part of the words they phonographically express. as "417 *meaning* comfortable"; 4G, *meaning* "foregoing"; wndr5- wonderfully: rt-J artfulness. Grammalogues that take s to form their plural require a space *after* the s, but no space before the grammalogues, 'housWRs ntl ystrD; *meaning* "the house was ours until yesterday." (Note space between Rs and ntl.)

If we except the small letters, c, n, o, p, x, and initial capital letters of proper names and prefixes, it may be taken as a rule without an exception, that wherever a grammalogue, suffix, punctuation mark or figure, used as an abbreviation as also a vowel, occurs, there will be no space *before* or *after* such character.

The punctuation marks " ; . ? retain their normal use. The semi-colon (;) and inverted commas ("") when used for punctuation, have a *space* to the left; when used as prefixes, there is no *space*.

EXPLANATORY.

The chief impediment to fast typewriting is the frequent use of the spacer or space key, which requires a tap of the finger just like a letter of the alphabet, and is consequently very tedious where words of one syllable occur. The system of stenotypy is based on the principal of elimination, or getting rid of space whenever this economy does not cause confusion in the reading of the subject matter. Accordingly the author has found it expedient to group, under the headings of grammalogues, prefixes and suffixes, the words of most frequent use in the language, especially those words and suffixes difficult to be read without vowels. It must be carefully borne in mind that wherever a grammalogue, figure, stop, suffix or capital vowel occurs, there must be no space either before or after the next letter. All these when used as abbreviations, as also vowels indicate *space* (or the end of a word) as readily as a blank which requires the tap of a spacer. Prefixes must have one space to the left, except the inverted commas, and semi-colon, which have no space to the left or right.

VOWELS, ETC.

The capital vowels when used retain their long sounds : A, in alms, ale, all ; E, in eel ; I, in ice and oil ; O, in ode , U, in pure, food. The dipthongs oi, ou, oo, au, are expressed by small vowels. There must be no space before or after capital vowels.

The small or short vowels, a. e, i, o, u, are seldom used in words of more than one syllable and *never* when silent. Each of the small short vowels is expressed in the words: pat, pet, pit, pot, put.

The sound of each word is expressed, as in short hand systems, either phonetically or stenographically, either way being adopted inasmuch as it facilitates the *reading* of the exercise.

All consonants, vowels, and figures, such as B, C, I, K, T, 2, 4, 8, etc., stand for the words they phonetically express, C for see or sea, I for eye or I, T for tea, 2 for too or two, 8 for ate or eight, etc. IOU&$&&hlf means I owe you a dollar and a half. No regard need be paid to orthographic or correct spelling, only such words as may be considered indispensably necessary to give the sound of the word, must be expressed. As in all phonographic systems, each word expressed by consonants, must be guessed by supplying vowels, or from its position in the context. The reader, after a little practice, will find no difficulty in making out the words expressed by their consonants, as bsk, bbl, bkm, drk, meaning bask or busk, became or become, dark or dirk. The context will readily suggest the word that is meant.

When it is necessary to prefix a capital letter to a word, the capital is prefixed to the word with a space before it as r@,2 Jms& Ptr, " write to James and Peter."

EXERCISES ON THE
GRAMMALOGUES, PREFIXES, SUFFIXES, FIGURES AND STOPS.

B   Bst&. BBDntC (rZNy(.2BCn wr(yFntg.

Be standing by, but do not say there is anything to be seen worthy of notice.

C   HWhsCn' Mdtrnn hsCn'lrgstFCs.

He who has seen the Mediterranean has seen the largest of seas.

D   ddNy&Cwn Grg ddFpplxy?

Did anyone say when George died of apoplexy?

F   Drn$ (s brn$FOkF'trEFUR7BcsTZrtn.

Do wrench this branch of oak off the tree, if you are able, because it is rotten.

G   HLG2$&prA2GWlvs mnNVG.

He will go to church and pray to God who loves man in every age.

H J   HLntHHprA2JbksHW&J.

He will not have him pray to Jesus because he was a Jew.

H J   FHHtrUGldJHwd wrJG.

If he have true godliness he would worship God.

K   'hpJF'blsdNhvnKmnKK.

The happiness of the blessed in heaven no man can know.

L   'LLhrLWprA2H.

The Lord will hear all who pray to him.

M   UMbr.MM$r4lMtrdFwlk,.

You may bring me my chair, for I am tired of walking.

N   IMN&ngn-stt6N'tpF(s hl.

I am in an ungainly situation on the top of this hill.

P   Nv@ 'P2cm&pA(r dUsB4TLB2lS.

Invite the people to come and pay their dues before it will be too late.

Q   'QWtndd'QWQ-rmvd4slvnJFwrkmnJ.

The quack who attended the queen was quickly removed for slovenness of workmanship.

R   (rR5oR&hndrdF'RmnN'mpl7FR JOns.

There are fifty or a hundred of our men in the employment of Mr. Jones.

S   SSnt DSsn.

She shall not die so soon.

T   TprtFTZTF'qst6.

That part of it is out of the question.

U   UwrLrdmdB'bldFJXRL&svr.

You were all redeemed by the blood of Jesus Christ, our Lord and Saviour.

V	Vmn smsVgd ntlUfndTyr mst / .
	Every man seems very good until you find out your mistake.
W	WLsstSn-W(sWRvrt:.
	We will associate only with those who are virtuous.
X	XWN x prsn n 'htrdF'Js.
	Christ was an extraordinary person, notwithstanding the hatred of the Jews.
Y	WwrLrdmdBYOXfrYmrcyZbyndUmn nlG.
	We were all redeemed by Thee, O Christ, for thy mercy is beyond human knowledge.
Z	YLBdnNr(ZTZNhvn.
	Thy will be done on earth as it is in heaven.
$	$ldJ&OldGR'2xtrmsFl5.
	Childhood and old age are the two extremes of life.
(	I(tlWG,2ps (rU'gS.
	I thought I was going to pass through the gate.
)	')pWsbmrgd.
	The ship was submerged.
1	IH2Is.
	I have two eyes.
2	I Hxmnd hs2Is&fndYwr2lng nglktd.
	I have examined his two eyes and find they were too long neglected.
3	m3cn3mm3.
	Marry, country, memory.
4	(r4k,4.
	Therefore, kingdom.
5	bn5str5.
	Baneful, strife.
6	Hl5sN'mn6H6.
	He lives in the mansion himself.
7	ncp7Fmprv7.
	Incapable of improvement.
8	'pr8hs n(r prb8nr4t8.
	The pirate has neither probity nor fortitude.
9	TZEsv2dtkt pIr9N'srf9F9.
	It is easy to detect piracy on the surface of ice.
o	IOU&$&&hlf.
&	&boy&&mn gv$&$.
	A boy and a man gave each a dollar.
'	(comma over the line) 'mn&'wmn. The man and the woman.

.   (comma on the line)   'mnZsns-NhsNt / ,.

The man is senseless in his undertaking.

    (colon)   TW&glr : Dfr'crc :.

It was a glorious day for the circus.

–   (dash)   nh–lw–J.

Unholy lawlessness.

@   wr@.&n@X&mn@.

Write a note in a minute.

⧣   rm⧣ ;⧣@ LtIms.

Remember progress at all times.

%   TZsi%2$rg6%·

It is simony to charge six per cent.

—   Gbk__2m__.

Go backward to impart.

/   t/$mnl/H.

Take each man like him.

¢   TZpls¢2KThs rs¢vst cstB$50¢.

It is pleasant to know that his recent visit cost but one dollar and fifty cents.

    n ' x cs F(s p cAsWL n Nt/T.

Notwithstanding the extraordinary circumstances of this particular case, we will nevertheless, undertake it.

PREFIXES.

It must be borne in mind, that, unlike the *Affixes* and Grammalogues, (which require no space before or after), the *prefixes* herein inserted must have a *space* preceding, except the inverted commas and semi-colon which have no space. Thus IMG,2 2dktU. I am going to contradict you. The figure 2 is utilized to express *contra, contri, contro, counter.* But it must be observed there is a *space* between the two twos. This rule must be observed in all cases where prefixes are used, except in cases where the semi-colon (;) and inverted commas ("") are used, which have no space except when used as punctuation marks.

2	contra, contri, contro, counter. II 2m&s'rdr. He countermands the order.
3	enter, inter, intro, intru. IL 3dsU. I will introduce you.
4	magna, magne, magni. TZ 4fsċ. It is magnificent.
5	trans. II 5lSs Lvy. He translates Livy.
6	accom, accum, accoun. TZEsy2 6pl). It is easy to accomplish.
7	encom, incon, encoun, incog. TZV 7vEnÇ. It is very inconvenient.
8	recoun, recog. H SnIzdM. He recognized me.
9	retra, retre, retri, retro. TL 9v. It will retrieve.
%	circum. 'cptn %nvg8s. The captain circumnavigates.
#	hypo, hyper. 'mnZ #krtkl. The man is hypocritical.
/	after, afore. HcAm / _s. He came afterwards.
"	H"&sM2r@. He commands me to write.
;	HZ& ;dċ ;sdċ. He is a prudent president.

READING EXERCISES

IN STENOTYPY.

The Lord's Prayer.

Rf (rWRtNhvn hlwdBYnmYk. 4 cmYLBdnNr(ZTZNhvn g5Z(sDRD–brd&4g5 ZRtrspsZW4g5(sWtrsps gnstZ&lEdZntN2tmpt6BdlvrZfrm vl. Mn.

Our Father who art in heaven, hallowed be thy name, thy kingdom come, thy will be done on earth as it is in heaven; give us this day our daily bread and forgive us our trespasses, as we forgive those who trespass against us, and lead us not into temptation but deliver us from evil.   Amen.

The Lord's Prayer written in full requires that the letter keys and spacer be struck 283 times; whilst according to Stenotypy only 116 taps are necessary.

The following extracts will immediately represent to the eye the advantages of Stenotypy over ordinary typewriting.

From Addison's "Tattler."

I$nsd2rIsVr-& p mrn, (s smr&t/&wlkN2'cn32'dvrtM6mng'fld s&mdws wl'grnWnw&'flwrsNblm. ZT(s sEsnF'yrVlAnZ& bUt5wlk& Vhdg5Fns gs IlstM6W&gr8dlFpl)r mng svrl (kts&b)sTwr fldW& gr8vr8Fbrds&Ngr7cnf6FnOts w$4md'plsۊst sEnN' o 2&Whd psd &wOl wntrNnois&smk.

I chanced to rise very early one particular morning this summer, and took a walk into the country to divert myself among the fields and meadows while the green was new, and the flowers in bloom.   As at this season of the year every lane is a beautiful walk and every hedge full of nosegays, I lost myself with a great deal of pleasure among several thickets and bushes, that were filled with a variety of birds and an agreeable confusion of notes, which formed the pleasantest scene in the world to me, who had passed a whole winter in noise and smoke.

n(,mr5-ts ts'Ut18F)r t&r@t, (n'rpd8Ww$Ths grwnN2Ze dr
,'pst fUyrs. 50 yrsG&sk1d)r t&r@trWrAr&'r tW1kdPZ&srtF
ms3&S4md7Ftn7Z2dtrLB'mst crg:frm tempt,2f(mTs ms3s.

Nothing more fully attests the utility of shorthand writing than the rapidity with which it has grown into use during the past few years. Fifty years ago a skilled short-hand writer was rare, and the art was looked upon as a sort of mystery, and so formid-able of attainment as to deter all but the most courageous from attempting to fathom its mysteries.

To write the latter extract, the keys and spacer of a typewriting machine must be struck 150 times according to Stenotype; and 344 times according to the ordinary method. To write the same according to Pitman's phonography, 221 motions of the hand or pen are required; Munson's system 195, and Graham's 193. In the above extract, Stenotypy has a gain of 67 motions over Pitman's phonography, 41 over Munson's and 39 over Graham's. The gain of Stenotypy is there-fore a mathematical fact.

From "The Guardian."

'(rZKvr tUSt.r-gr8&G1/Zjst9. mstF'(r vrtsR'vrtsFcrt8d
B,R 68d2RntrZWRmn. jst9ZTW$Zprtk9dBGH6&2Bprtk9dNTs
prfk6BnnBH. ZTBprfk-jstZNtrb@F'dvn ntr2BS2'tmstFRbl8s
Z'g13Fmn. wn&n6&c lssTs rgrd4jst9wnYDnt lkPTZsm(,
vnr7&nvl7wnNyF(m dAr2;sm2lsn frntRtrfy (swH'dstrb6FT
N(r h&s wn&jdgZcp7FB,nflnsdBny(,B1wR&causMB 8nddBny(,
TZ4n2Ts wn mrtsWMvntr2;nns Ts$&n6Zhstn,2Ts rUn. 4
(s rsn'bst lw TVpsdNRDZTw$"tnsRjdgsN(r psts dr,(r gd
bhvrWT1v,(m2'mrcyFs$WNil tms mtBNndUnflnsV(m trbl&prvrt
'crsFjst9.

There is no virtue so truly great and God-like as justice. Most of the other virtues are the virtues of created beings or accommodated to our nature as we are men. Justice is that which is practiced by God himself, and to be practiced in its perfection by none but him. As to be perfectly just is an attribute of the divine nature to be so to the utmost of our abilities, is the glory of man. When a nation once loses its regard for justice; when they do not look upon it as something venerable and inviolable; when any of them dare to presume to lessen, affront or terrify those who have the distribution of it in their hands; when a judge is capable of being influenced by anything but law, or a cause may be recommended by anything that is foreign to its own merits, we may venture to pronounce that such a nation is hastening to its ruin. For this reason the best law that has ever passed in our day is that which continues our judges in their posts during their good behavior, without leaving them to the mercy of such, who in ill times, might by an undue influence over them trouble and pervert the course of justice.

From " Genesis."—Chapter I.

N' bgn, Gcr8d hvn&r (. &' r (WWT4m&void&drk JWP' f9F' dp.
&' spr tFGmvdP' f9F' wtrs&Gsd lt (rBl@&(rWl@. &Gsw' l@ TT
Wgd&Gdvdd' l@frm' drk J. &Gcld' ltD&' drk JHcld nIt. &'
vn, &'mrn, wr'frs tD. &Gsd lt (rB&frm7N'mds tF'wtrs. &Gmd'
frm7&dvdd'wtrs w$ wrN'frm7frm'wtrs w$ wr bv' frm7&TWS. &
Gcld'frm7hvn. &'vn, &'mrn, wr'skndD. &Gsd lt'wtrsNhvnB
g(rd2g(rN2&pls&lt'dry l&pr&TWS. &Gcld'dry l&r(&'g(r,
2g(rF'wtrsHcldCs&GswTTWgd. &Gsd lt'r(br, 4(grs'hrb yld,
sEd&'frt trE yld, frt ftrTs kndWs sdZNT6P'r(&TWS. &'r(brt
4(grs&hrb yld, sd ftrTs knd&'trEyld, frtWs sEdWNT6 ftrTs
knd&GswTTWgd. &'vn, &'mrn, wr'(rdD. &Gsd lt (rBltsN'frm7F
hvn2dvd'Dfrm'nt&lt (mB4sIns&4ssns&4Ds&yrs. &lt (m
B4ltsN'frm7Fhvn2g51tP'r(&TWS. &Gmd2gr8lts'gr8r lt2rl
'D&'lsr lt2rl'ntHmd'strsLS. &Gs t (mP'frm7Fhvn2g51tP'r(&2rU
10vr'D&vr'nt&2dvd'lt frm'drkJ&GswTTWgd. &'vn, &'mrn, wr'4 (D.
&Gsd lt'wtrs br, 4(bnd&- 'mv, cr trs TH15&'fwlTMAf-bv'r(N'Opn
frm7Fhvn. &Gcr8d gr8whls&Vlv, cr trTmv(w$'wtrs brt4(bnd
&-ftr(r knd&Vw, d fwl ftrTs knd&GswTTWgd. &'vn, &'mrn, wr'5(

D.   &Gsd 1 t Zm/ mnNRmG& f t r R1 k J&1 t HHdmn6V'f)F'C&V'fw1F'Ar
&V'ct1&VL'r(&VVcrp, (, Tcrp(P'r.   &Gb1sd (m&sdBfrt5&m1t
p-&rp1n)'r(&sbdUT&Hdmn8V'f)F'C&V'fw1F'Ar&VV1v, (, Tmv(P'r).

In the beginning God created heaven and earth ; and the earth was without form
and void, and darkness was upon the face of the deep. And the spirit of God moved
upon the face of the waters. And God said, let there be light and there was light.
And God saw the light that it was good, and God divided the light from the darkness.
And God called the light day ; and the darkness He called night. And the evening and
the morning were the first day. And God said let there be a firmament in the midst of
the waters. And God made the firmament and divided the waters which were under
the firmament from the waters which were above the firmament, and it was so. And
God called the firmament heaven. And the evening and the morning were the second
day. And God said, let the waters under heaven be gathered together unto one place,
and let dry land appear, and it was so. And God called the dry land earth, and the
gathering together of the waters He called seas, and God saw that it was good. And
God said, let the earth bring forth grass, the herb yielding seed, and the fruit tree yielding fruit after its kind, whose seed is in itself upon the earth, and it was so. And the
earth brought forth grass, and herb yielding seed after its kind, and the tree yielding
fruit after its kind whose seed was in itself, after its kind upon the earth ; and God saw
that it was good. And the evening and the morning were the third day. And God
said, let there be lights in the firmament of heaven to divide the day from the night, and
let them be for signs and for seasons, and for days and years. And let them be for
lights in the firmament of heaven to give light upon the earth, and it was so. And God
made two great lights, the greater light to rule the day and the lesser light to rule the
night ; He made the stars also. And God set them upon the firmament of heaven, to
give light upon the earth. And to rule over the day and over the night and to divide
the light from the darkness, and God saw that it was good. And the evening and the
morning were the fourth day. And God said, let the waters bring forth abundantly the
moving creatures that have life, and fowl that may fly above the earth in the open firmament of heaven. And God created great whales and every living creature that moveth
which the waters brought forth abundantly after their kind, and every winged fowl
after its kind, and God saw that it was good. And the evening and the morning were
the fifth day. And God said, let us make man in our image and after our likeness, and
let him have dominion over the fishes of the sea, and over the fowl of the air, and over
the cattle, and over all the earth and over every creeping thing upon the earth. And
God blessed them and said, be fruitful and multiply, and replenish the earth and subdue
it, and have dominion over the fish of the sea, and over the fowl of the air, and over
every living thing that moveth upon the earth.

Rich and Rare Were the Gems She Wore.—*Moore*.

r$&rAr wr´gmsSwOr
&&br@gld r,Nhr w&SbOr
BOhr bUtyWfr bOnd
hr sprkl,gms&snOwlt W&.

Sr n@IfEl nt'lEst lrm
KsnF ErnLOfrMArm
4L(OYlv wmn&gldn stOr
sr n@Ylv hnr&vrtUmr.

ldy dstYnt fEr2strA
(rU(s lOn&blEk wA?
R Erns snsSgUdRScld
Znt2BtmtdBwmnRgld?

NSw&&hr mdns smll
Nsfty l@d hr rnd'grEnll
&blst4VWSWrld
N Erns Onr& Erns prld.

Rich and rare were the gems she wore,
And a bright gold ring on her wand she
bore:
But O her beauty was far beyond
Her sparkling gems and snow white wand.

Sir Knight, I feel not the least alarm,
No son of Erin will offer me harm ;
For, although they love women and golden
store,
Sir Knight they love honor and virtue more.

Lady, dost thou not fear to stray
Through this lone and bleak way ?
Are Erin's sons so good or so cold
As not to be tempted by women or gold ?

On she went, and her maiden's smile
In safety alighted her around the green Isle,
And blest forever was she who relied
On Erin's honor and Erin's pride.

They Know Not My Heart.—*Moore*.

YKntMhrtWblv (rKB
&stAnF(s r(NT= fl,s4Y
W(nk wllCYNbUtys yng hr
ZpUrZ´mrn,frst dUN'flwr
lcd hrm wtllvZ´sns w&n rA
BsmlsN'dUdrp2wstTwA.

Kbm,Wl@Z(s yng fEtrsR
(rZ&l@rndYhrt w$Zlvlr fr
TZntT$EkTZ´sOl dwn,clEr
(rUts n&bl) m∕sYbUtySdr
Z´skyWlkP2(Oglr:&fAr
Z´lkdP2´mrBcAs hvnZ(r.

They know not my heart, who believe
there can be
One stain of this earth in its feelings for
thee ;
Who think, while I see thee in beauty's
young hour.

As pure as the morning's first dew on the
flower,
I could harm what I love—as the sun's
wanton ray
But smiles on the dewdrop to waste it
away !

No—beaming with light as those young
  features are,
There's a light round thy heart which is
  lovelier far ;
It is not that cheek—'tis the soul dawning
  clear

Through its innocent blush makes thy
  beauty so dear—
As the sky we look up to, though glorious
  and fair,
Is looked up to the more, because heaven
  is there !—*Moore*.

Mb@ZN')ORMbrkZN'C
BB4 IG Tm MOr hErZ&dbl hl(2Y
hEr Z&s I4 (sWlvM&&smI l4 (sW
  h8
&wtVsky ZbvMhErZ&hr t4Vf8.

My boat is on the shore,
  My bark is on the sea,
But before I go, Tom Moore,
  Here's a double health to thee.

Here's a sigh for those who love me,
  And a smile for those who hate,
And whatever sky is above me,
  Here's a heart for every fate.—*Byron*.

In no system of shorthand invented by man could the above extract be written more legibly
and in less characters. While no word signs are used that are not authorized by standard phonography, it requires but 90 taps in Stenotypy against 220 taps or motions of the hand when
written in full.

ÆSOP'S FABLES.

The Miller, His Son, and Their Ass.

Amlr&hs sn wr drv, (rAs2&nbr, fAr2s1H.   Yhd nt gn fr
wnYmtW&trpFwmn clktd rnd&wl tlk,&lf,.   lk (r crd&F(m dd
UVCs$ flOs2Btrg, lng'rdNft wnYmt rId? 'ld mn hr, (s qk-md
hs sn mnt'As& "tnd2wlk lng mr-Bhs s@. ;snt-YcmP2&grpF
ld mnNrnst db8.   (r sd&T ;vs wtIWC,.   wt rspktZ)n2
ldGN(sDs? DUCTIdl ld rd,wl hs ld f(r hs2wlk? gt dwnU
yng skpgr9&lt'ld mn rst hs w3lms. P(s'ld mn m8hs sn dsmt
&gtPH6. N(s mnrYhd nt ;cdd fr wnYmt& "pnyFwmn&$ldrn.

wIU19yOld flOcrd svrl tngsT&c hw cnUr@P'bst wITpr ltl
ld (rKhr-kp p9B's@FU? 'gdn8rd mlr md8-tkPhs snBhndH.
Yhd nwLmst r$d'twn. ;hnst frnd sd&ctznZTAsUrOn? ys sd
'ld mn O&wld ntH(tSsd'(rB'wAUldH. wIU2flOsRbtr72c3'pr
bst (nHU. &(,2plsUsd'ld mnWcnB3. Sallt,Whs snYtId'lgsF'
As2g(r&B'hlpF&plNdvrd2c3HN(r)ldrsV&brg nr'ntrnsF'twn.
(s 3tn,S@br@'PNcrds21fTT. 'As nt lk,'nois nr'strng&l,
THW%jkt2ork'crdsTbndH&tml,F'pl flN2'wtr. P(s'ld mn vxd
&)md m@'bstFhs wAOm gn "vncdTBNdvr,2plsVbdyHhd plsd
Kbdy&lst hsAsN2'brgn.

A miller and his son were driving their Ass to a neighboring fair to sell him. They
had not gone far when they met with a troop of women, collected round a well, talk-
ing and laughing. "Look there," cried one of them, "did you ever see such fellows, to
be trudging along the road on foot, when they might ride?" The old man hearing this
quickly made his son mount the Ass, and continued to walk along merrily by his side.
Presently they came up to a group of old men in earnest debate. "There," said one of
them, "it proves what I was saying. What respect is shown to old age in these days?
Do you see that idle lad riding, while his old father has to walk? Get down, you
young scapegrace, and let the old man rest his weary limbs." Upon this the old man
made his son dismount, and got up himself. In this manner they had not proceeded
far when they met a company of women and children: "Why, you lazy old fellow,"
cried several tongues at once. "how can you ride upon the beast, while that poor little
lad there can hardly keep pace by the side of you?" The good-natured miller immediately took up his son behind him. They had now almost reached the town.
"Pray, honest friend," said a citizen, "Is that Ass your own?" "Yes," says the
old man. "O, one would not have thought so," said the other, "by the way you load
him. Why, you two fellows are better able to carry the poor beast than he you."
"Anything to please you," said the old man; "we can but try." So, alighting with
his son, they tied the legs of the Ass together, and by the help of a pole endeavored to
carry him on their shoulders over a bridge near the entrance of the town. This enter-
taining sight brought the people in crowds to laugh at it. The Ass, not liking the
noise, nor the strange handling that he was subject to, broke the cords that bound him,
and, tumbling off the pole, fell into the water. Upon this, the old man, vexed and
ashamed, made the best of his way home again, convinced that by endeavoring to please
everybody he had pleased nobody, and lost his Ass into the bargain.

The Father and His Sons.

Aſ(r hd&ſm-FsnsWwr prpt-qrl,mng(m6s. wnHſld2hl (r
dsp@sBhs xr t.6sHdtrmnd2g5(m&prctkl lstr6F'vlsFdsn6&4(s
prpsH&Dtld (m2br, H&bndlFstks. wnYhd dnSHpl9d'ſgtN2'h&sF
$F(m&rdrd (m2brkTNpcs. Y$trdWL(r strn(&wr nt72DT. Hnxt
unclsd'ſgt&tk'stks spr8-&B&&gn pt (mN2(r h&sNw Ybrk (m
Es-. H(n drsd (mN(s wrds. MsnsFURF&mnd&Un@2sst$o(rUL
BZ(s ſgtBFURdvdd mngUr6sULBbrknZEs-Z(s stks.

A father had a family of sons who were perpetually quarreling among themselves.
When he failed to heal their disputes by his exhortations, he determined to give them a
practical illustration of the evils of disunion; and for this purpose he one day told them
to bring him a bundle of sticks. When they had done so, he placed the faggot into the
hands of each of them in succession, and ordered them to break it in pieces. They
each tried with all their strength, and were not able to do it. He next unclosed the
faggot, and took the sticks separately, one by one, and again put them into their hands,
on which they broke them easily. He then addressed them in these words: " My
sons, if you are of one mind, and unite to assist each other, you will be as this faggot,
uninjured by all the attempts of your enemies; but if you are divided among yourselves,
you will be broken as easily as these sticks."

The Dog in the Manger.

Adg lAN&mngr&Bhs grwl, &snp, ;v&d'xn ſrmEt, 'hAw$ hd bn
pl9d4(m. wt&6) dg sd&F(m2hs "pn6sHcntEt'hAH6&yt rſss2lw
(sWK.

A Dog lay in a manger, and by his growling and snapping prevented the oxen from
eating the hay which had been placed for them. " What a selfish Dog!" said one of
them to his companions: " he cannot eat the hay himself, and yet refuses to allow those
to eat who can."

The Wolf in Sheep's Clothing.

&sP&tIm&wlſ rslvd2dsg9hs n8rBhs hbtTSHmt gt ſdWTst
&. NcsdN'sknF&)p HpstrdW'ſlkBgl, ')prdBhs rtſ9. N'vn,HW)tP

B')prdN'fld'g8Wclsd&'ntrns m8(r-skr.   ')prd cm, N2'fld dr,'nt2
¡v@.fd+'mrOcautP'wlfNstdF&)p&kldHWhs nfN'fld.   hrm sEk hrm fnd.

Once upon a time a Wolf resolved to disguise his nature by his habit, that so he
might get food without stint. Encased in the skin of a sheep, he pastured with the
flock, beguiling the shepherd by his artifice. In the evening he was shut up by the
shepherd in the fold : the gate was closed, and the entrance made thoroughly secure.
The shepherd coming into the fold during the night to provide food for the morrow,
caught up the Wolf, instead of a sheep, and killed him with his knife in the fold.

Harm seek, harm find.

The Lion in Love.

AliNdm&d'dtrF&wdctrNmrG.   'f(r nL, 2gr&&yt frd2rfshs
rqst htP(s xpd&2rdH6Fhs mprtnts.   Hxprsd hsL, J2cptHZ'
sUtrFhs dtrN&''d6TH)d lwH2xtrkt hs t(&ctFhs clwsZhs
dtrWfrf-frdFb(.   'liN$rf-s&d2';ps1 wn hvrHnxt rptd hs
rqst'wdmnKlngr frd stPHWhs clb&drvHwAN2'4st.

A Lion demanded the daughter of a wood-cutter in marriage. The father, unwill-
ing to grant, and yet afraid to refuse his request, hit upon this expedient to rid himself
of his importunities. He expressed his willingness to accept him as the suitor of his
daughter on one condition ; that he should allow him to extract his teeth, and cut off his
claws, as his daughter was fearfully afraid of both. The Lion cheerfully assented to the
proposal ; when, however, he next repeated his request, the woodman, no longer afraid,
set upon him with his club, and drove him away into the forest.

The Ass and the Mule.

AmltEr st+(N&jrny drv,B4H&As&&mU1 b(w1 ldn.   'As
ZlngZHtrvld lng'pln crd hs ldWEZBwnHbgn2s&'stp p(F'mntn
Hflt hs ld2Bmr (nHcd br.   Hntrtd hs"pn62rlvHF&sml pr6
THmt c30m'rstB'mU1 pdKtn62'rqst.   'As)rt-∕_sfl dwn ddNhs
brdn.   'mltEr ntK, wt els2DNSwld&rg6p19dP'mU1'ld crdB'AsN

24

d6²hsOn&T'tpFLp19d'hdF`As ╱Hhd ʃlAdH.　'mU1 grOn, bn(hs
hvy brdn sd (s2H6.　IMtrtd crd, ²Mdᵴrts.　ҒIhdN-BnL, 2ss t
'As&1tlNhs nEdI)d nt nwBbr, tg(rWhs brdnH6Zwl.

A muleteer set forth on a journey, driving before him an Ass and a Mule, both
well-laden. The Ass, as long as he traveled along the plain, carried his load with ease ;
but when he began to ascend the steep path of the mountain, he felt his load to be more
than he could bear.　He entreated his companion to relieve him of a small portion,
that he might carry home the rest ; but the Mule paid no attention to the request.　The
Ass shortly afterwards fell down dead under his burden.　The muleteer, not knowing
what else to do in so wild a region, placed upon the Mule the load carried by the Ass
in addition to his own, and at the top of all placed the hide of the Ass, after he had
flayed him.　The Mule, groaning beneath his heavy burden, said thus to himself :　" I
am treated according to my deserts.　If I had only been willing to assist the Ass a little
in his need, I should not now be bearing together with his burden, himself as well."

The Fox Who Had Lost His Tail.

Aʃx cautN&trp scpdW'lsFhs br(.　hns4(ʃ1, 15&brdn ʃrm
')m&rdk12w$HWxpsdHskEmd2br, L'(r ʃxsN2&1,　"d6WH6TN'"n
1sH mt'btr"s1 hs On dpr56.　Hsmbld&gd mny ʃxs&pb1k-dvsd
(m2ct (r t1sC, TYwd ntN-1k m$ btrWT(mBTYwd gt rdF'wtF'br(
w$W&Vgr8 7vnEns.　&F(m 3rpt, HsdFUhd ntUr61stUr t1Mʃrȶ
Uwd nt (s cns1Z.

A Fox caught in a trap, escaped with the loss of his " brush."　Henceforth feel-
ing his life a burden from the shame and ridicule to which he was exposed, he schemed
to bring all the other Foxes into a like condition with himself, that in the common loss
he might the better conceal his own deprivation.　He assembled a good many Foxes,
and publicly advised them to cut off their tails, saying, " that they would not only look
much better without them, but that they would get rid of the weight of the brush,
which was a very great inconvenience "　One of them interrupting him said : " If you
had not yourself lost your tail, my friend, you would not thus counsel us."

The Widow and the Sheep.

Acrtn pr wdOhd&s1t3)p.　T)r, tm w), ²t╱hs ʃlEs&2vd
xpnsS)rdHhr6BUsd')rsSnsk15-TW'ʃlsS)rd'ʃ1).　')p wr(, Wpn sd

wIDUhrtMSmstrs? wt wAt KMbld ad2'wl? FUw₵Mfl) (rℤ'b$rWL
klMN&tr9BFUw₵Mfls&wl (rℤ')rrWL)r&nt hrtM.
  'lEstTlAℤntLws'gr8st gn.

A certain poor widow had one solitary Sheep. At shearing time, wishing to take
his fleece. and to avoid expense, she sheared him herself, but used the shears so unskill
fully. that with the fleece she sheared the flesh. The Sheep, writhing with pain, said:
" Why do you hurt me so. mistress? What weight can my blood add to the wool? If
you want my flesh. there is the butcher, who will kill me in a trice ; but if you want my
fleece and wool. there is the shearer, who will shear and not hurt me."
  The least outlay is not always the greatest gain.

The Wild Boar and the Fox.

  Awld bOr stdN&trE&rbd hs tsks gnst'trnk. &fx ps,B
skdHwIH(s)rpnd hs t(wn (rWKdngr (rtn, frm (r hntsmnR
hnd. IIrpldIDTdvsd-4Twd nvrD2II2)rpnMwpns jstT'tmIOt2B
Us,(m. ₂Bwl;prd4wrZ'bst grntEFpEs.

A wild Boar stood under a tree, and rubbed his tusks against the trunk. A Fox
passing by, asked him why he thus sharpened his teeth when there was no danger
threatening from either huntsman or hound. He replied: " I do it advisedly ; for it
would never do to have to sharpen my weapons just at the time I ought to be using
them."
  To be well prepared for war is the best guarantee of peace.

The Ass Carrying the Image.

  &as&c crd (rU'strtsF&c8&fms wdn mG2Bp19dN&FTs tm
pls. 'crwdZIlpsd lng m8lw-;str6B4'mG. 'as (nk, TYbwd (r
hdsNtknFrspkt4II6brsldPWprd&gvII6Ars&rfsd2mv n(r stp. '
drvrC,II(s stp ld hs whp lst-bt hs)ldrs&sd0Uprvrs dl hd
Tℤnt yt cm2(sTmn pAwrJ2&as.
  YRnt wIsWt⁄2(m6s'crdt dU2(rs.

An Ass once carried through the streets of a city a famous wooden image, to be
placed in one of its Temples. The crowd as he passed along made lowly prostration

before the image. The Ass, thinking that they bowed their heads in token of respect for himself, bristled up with pride and gave himself airs, and refused to move another step. The driver seeing him thus stop, laid his whip lustily about his shoulders, and said : "O you perverse dull-head! it is not yet come to this, that men pay worship to an Ass."

They are not wise who take to themselves the credit due to others.

The Ass and His Masters.

&asBlng, 2&hrbslrWgvII21tl fd&2m$ wrk m8&pt62 JptrT
IIwd rlsIIfrm hs;snt srv9&; vdIIW&(r mstr. Jptr/wrn, HTH
wd rp¢hs rqst cAsdH2Bsld2&tIlmkr.)rt-/_s fnd, THhd hvr
10ds2c3&hrdr wrkN'brk fldHpt6d4n(rmstr. Jptr tl, HTT)dB'
lst tImTIIcd gr¢hs rqst rdndTII)dBsld2&tnr. 'as fnd, TIIhd
flnN2wrs&s&nOt, hs mstrs ocp6sd grOn, TwdIIBn btr4M2IIBn
strvdB'&R2HBnVwrkdB'(rFM4mr mstrs (n2HBn bOtBM;s¢OnrWL
Evn/IMdd tnMhId&m/MUs-2II.

An Ass belonging to an herb-seller, who gave him too little food and too much work, made a petition to Jupiter that he would release him from his present service, and provide him with another master. Jupiter, after warning him that he would repent his request, caused him to be sold to a tile-maker. Shortly afterwards, finding that he had heavier loads to carry, and harder work in the brick-field, he petitioned for another master. Jupiter, telling him that it should be the last time that he could grant his request, ordained that he should be sold to a tanner. The Ass finding that he had fallen into worse hands, and noting his master's occupation, said, groaning : " It would have been better for me to have been either starved by the one, or to have been over-worked by the other of my former masters, than to have been bought by my present owner, who will even after I am dead tan my hide, and make me useful to him."

The Brother and the Sister.

Af(r hd&sn&&dtr'4mr rmrkd74hs gd lks'ltr4hr x uglJ. wl
Ywr pl, &DZ$1drnYhpndB$ns21kN2&mrrTWpl9dN(r m(rs $r. 'boy
"grtlSdII6Nhs gd lks'grl grw&gry&cd nt br'6prssFhr br(r 3

prt, LIIsd&hw cdSD(rws?N2rf1x6Nhr6. SrnF2hrf(r2BrvngdN
hr trnNhr br(r&sp@5- cU=dIIFII, %&by m8UsFTw$n-blngs2grls.
ï(r mbr9d (m b(&bs tw, hs kss&fk6m_)-N$sdIw)Ub(VD21kN2'mrr
UMsnTUMnt splUr bUtyBEv1"dct&UMdtr TUMm⁄P4Urwéfbty B
Ur vrts.

A father had one son and one daughter ; the former remarkable for his good looks,
the latter for her extraordinary ugliness. While they were playing one day as children
they happened by chance to look together into a mirror that was placed on their
mother's chair. The boy congratulated himself on his good looks : the girl grew angry,
and could not bear the self-praises of her brother ; interpreting all he said (and how
could she do otherwise?) into reflection on herself. She ran off to her father, to be
avenged in her turn on her brother, and spitefully accused him of having, as a boy,
made use of that which belonged only to girls. The father embraced them both, and
bestowing his kisses and affection impartially on each, said : " I wish you both every
day to look into the mirror ; you, my son, that you may not spoil your beauty by evil
conduct ; and you, my daughter, that you may make up for your want of beauty by
your virtues. '

STORY OF THE ALPS.

(rZ&t$, st3t0ldN'tmpl mgzEnB Rev. R. H. ConwelF&vst
2'hsptlF St. Brnrd wrRkpt'wndr5 St. Brnrd dgsFWs wrkF
rskU, trvlrsVt,⁄nB' AlpIn strmsSmnytAlsRfmlr2L. &mrn, ⁄
&stOrm sys d Cnwell &F(s gr8hnst crEtrs.cAm strgl, (rU'
snOhmprd gr8-Nhs xhstd"d6B'mntr brlFbr&yThng2hs clr. I
wAdd dEpN'drfts flw, 'flndr, Ol flOrnd'hsp92'knl w$W&rUmF
"sdr7sIz. wn'dOrW0pnd2'w&rr'(r dgsWNs tP&$OrsFbrks&whIns
&flV&n(rZYcrwdd btH&Egr-flwdHrndWwgsF(r tAls&nqst5lks
N(rIs w$ wr jstZntlg&qs6, ZSm&y 30gt6pnts. B'crstfln
bEst hld hs hd&tA12'flOr&snEkd bt frm&crnr2n(r&fIn-1A
dwn pc, N&drk n$N'stOn bs7. HlA(rWhsIs glns, TT'crnrsN&
mst)Am5wA. 'yng mnk cld'wE3dgBnAm&wn'bEst wld nt 1Ev
hs)dOy rtrt'prEst trd2ndUsH2"4(B)0, H&d)"tn, skrpsFmEt.
Bhng3%HWHmr-0pnd hsIs&ltl wldr rpd'flOr&cR291It-%Hgv&

·8

fEbl wAg2hs tAl&(n)rnk bk&sEmd nt2hEr'n@A6. 'mp)çkEpr
trnd wAW&ngry gstr&sdT'dg wd gtVhs slks sUn&T'crEtr;b7-
flt)AmdTHhd nt fnd&y&. '(t-rmrk)tN2MsO1W&(rl. TnObl
O1 flOsEmd2HfltSbdS)AmdRSgltyBcausHhd rtrndWTsAv, &y&TH
cd ntEt. TWnt hs fAltTKBnItd w&rr hdBnTBnmd&dy, N'mntn
rOdTA5nIt. Hhd gr&-dn hs dUtyBHWjst dg nuf nt2rsnSfr&
jstUm&nuf2fEITTWhs mpr85dUty2sAv sm&. gr&O1 f1O. hwH
Aut2pt2)Am m&y&Umn sO1WKs (rRtrv1rsG, dwnN'bIt, cO1d&'Vwlm,
strmsF15s mntn; hIwAs&y tWnvr sAvd Evn&s$.

There is a touching story told in the Temple Magazine, by Rev. Dr. R. H. Conwell,
of a visit to the hospital of St. Bernard, where are kept the wonderful St. Bernard dogs,
of whose work of rescuing perishing travelers overtaken by the Alpine storms so many
tales are familar to all. " One morning after a storm," says Dr. Conwell, " one of
those great, honest creatures came struggling through the snow, hampered greatly in
his exhausted condition by the miniature barrel of brandy that hung to his collar. I
waded deep in the drifts following the floundering old fellow around the hospice to the
kennel, which was a room of considerable size. When the door was opened to the
wanderer, the other dogs within set up a chorus of barks and whines, and fell over one
another as they crowded about him, and eagerly followed him around with wags of
their tails and inquisitive looks in their eyes, which were just as intelligent questionings
as so many interrogation points. But the crestfallen beast held his head and tail to the
floor, and sneaked about from one corner to the other, and finally lay down panting in a
dark niche in the stone basement. He lay there, with his eyes glancing out at the
corners, in a most shamefaced way. The young monk called the weary dog by name,
and when the beast would not leave his shadowy retreat, the priest tried to induce him
to come forth by showing him a dish containing scraps of meat. But, hungry as he was,
he merely opened his eyes a little wider, rapped the floor once or twice lightly, as he
gave a feeble wag to his tail, and then shrank back and seemed not to hear the invitation. The impatient keeper turned away with an angry gesture, and said that the dog
would ' get over his sulks very soon,' and that the creature probably felt ashamed that
he ' had not found any one.'

" The thoughtless remark shot into my deepest soul with a thrill. That noble old
fellow seemed to have felt so bad, so ashamed or so guilty because he had returned
without saving any one that he could not eat. It was not his fault that no benighted
wanderer had been out benumbed and dying on the mountain road that awful night. He
had grandly done his duty ; but he was just dog enough not to reason so far, and just

29

human enough to feel that it was his imperative duty to save some one. Grand old fellow! How he ought to put to shame many a human soul who knows there are travelers going down in the biting cold and the overwhelming storms of life's mountainous highways, and yet who never saved even one such!"—*The Observer.*

Declaration of Independence.

wnN'cOrsFUmn v¢sTBcms nss34&P2dslv'pltcl b¢s w$II"ctd (mWN(r&2sUm mng'pwrsF'r('spr8&Eql st62w$'lwsFn8r&n8rsG nt@1 (m&ds¢rspct2'pnn6sFmnknd rqrsTY)d dclr'cAss w$ mpl (m2'-t16

WO1d (s tr(s2B6vd¢. TLmnRcr8dEql. TYRndwdB(r cr8rW crtn nAln7r@sTmng (sR151brty&'prstFhpJ. T2scUr (s r@s gvr7sRnst@d mng mn drv, (r jst pwrs frm'"s¢F'gvrndTwnvr &y4mFgvr7Bcms dstrct5F(s ndsTZ'r@F'P2LtrRbl)T&2ns tt@& nUgvrn71A, Ts fnd6Ns$ prnspls&rgnz, Ts pwrsNs$4m%2(mSsm mst 1'-2fkt (r sfty&hpJ. ¡dés nddLdct8Tgvr7 lng stbl)d)d ntB$ngd41@& 5i¢cAss&crd, -Lxprns h( )nTmnkndRmr dspsd 2sfr wll Evl-Rsfr7(n2r@(m6sBbl), '4ms2w$YRcstmd. Bwn&lng trnFbUss&srpA6s prs, Nvr7-'sm bjkt vncs&ds12rdU ¢s(mN bsl@dsptsmT%(r r@TZ(r dty2(r0Fs$ gvr7&2¡ vd nUgrds4(r ftr scr8. s$ hsBn'p)csfrnsF(s clns&s$%nw'nss8w$"strns (m2 Ltr (r 4mr sstmsFgvrn7. 'hst3F'¡s¢k, Fgr8 BrtnZ&hst3Frptd njrs&Usrp6sLH, Ndrct bjkt'stbl)7F&bsl@tyrnyV(s st8s. 2¡v (-1t fct-B %mtd2&cndd o .

Hhs rfUsd hs s¢21ws'mstOlsm&nss34'pblc gd.

Hhslbdn hs gvrnrs2ps lwsFmd8&prs, mprt&s n-ssp¢ddN(r pr6tl hs sc)dBbtnd. &wnSsspcddHhs tr-nglctd2tnd2(m. Hhs rfUsd2ps (r lws4' 6d6Flrg dstrctsFPn-(sPwd rlnq) 'r@Frprset6N 'lgsurr&r@nsow72(m&4md72tyr¢s n-.

Hhs cld2g)r lgs185bdsTp19s nU)l n'47&dstéfrm'rpst3F' pblc rcrds4'sO1 prpsFftg, (mWhs m)rs.

Hhs ds1vd rprsȼ85hss rptd-4ps, Wmn-frJhs nvsGN'r@sF'P.

Hhs rfsd4&1ng tm,⁄s$ ds162cAs (rs2B1ctd wrB'1gs185pwrs ncp7Fnh16Hrtrnd2'PT1rg4(r xrcs'st8rmn, N'mntm xpsd2L'dngrs FnvsGfrmWT&"v1s6s frmWN.

Hhs ndvrd2; vȼ'pp16F(s st8s4Tprps bstrct, 'lwsFntr1z6F 4nrs rfs, 2ps (rs2ncrG(r mgr6h(r&rs, '"d6sFnUprpr6sF1&s.

Hhs bstrctd'dmnstr86Fjst9Brfs, hs sȼ21ws4stb1), jdc3 pwrs.

Hhs m8jdgs dpȼdȼNhsL10n4'tnrF(r fcs&'mnt&pA7F(r s13s.

Hhs rctd&m1t8FnUfcs&sch(r swrmsFfcrs2hrsRP&EtT (r sbst&s.

Hhs kpt mngZNtmsFpEs st&, rmsWT'"sȼFR1gs18rs.

Hhs fktd2rndr'm1t3ndpndȼF&sprr2'cv1 pwr.

Hhs"bndW(rs2 %jktZ2&jrsdk64n2R"st@t6&ncn1GdBR1ws gv, hs sȼ2(r; tndd ctsF1gs16.

4qrtr, 1rg bds Frmd trps mngZ

4; tct, (mB&mck tr1 frm pn)74&y mrdrs w$Y)d"tN'nhbtȼs F(s st8s.

4ct, FRtrdWL_sF' o .

4mps, txsNZWTR"sȼ.

4dprv, ZNm&y cssF'bnftsFtr1Bjry.

4 5prt, Zbynd'Cs2Btrd4; tndd fnss.

4b1), 'frEsstmF Eng1) 1wsN&nbr, ; vns stb1), (rN&rbtr3 gvrn7&n1rg, Ts bnd3sSZ2rndrTT&c&xmp1&ft nstr7lntrds, ' sm bs1@r1N2(s c1ns.

4 tk, wAR$rtrs b1), Rmst v171ws&Ltr, fnd7-'4msFRgvrn7.

4sspnd, ROn 1gs18rs&dc1r, (m6nvstdWpwr21gs184ZNLcss wtvr.

Hhs bdc8d gvrn7hrBdc1r, ZTFhs; tk6&wg, wr gnstZ.

Hhs p1ndrdRCs rvGdRcsts brntRtwns&dstrd'15sFRP.

HZT(s tm 5prt, 1rg rmEsF4n mrcn3s2"p1t'wrksFd(ds16&

tyrnyLrdyBgnW o Fcrlty&prfdy scrc-prlldN'mst brbr:Gs&
t@-nwr(y`ndF&cv19d n6.

  Hhs·'strndRflOctzns t/n cpt5N'hICs2or rms gnst (r
cn32Bcm`xct6rsF(r frᶐs&br(rnR2fl (m6sB(r h&s.

  Hhs x@d dmstc nsrx6s mngZ&hs ndvrd2br,N'nhbtᶜFR
frntrs·mrc- Indn svGsWsnOn rlFwrfrZ&ndstng)d dstrc6FLGs
sxs&·d6s.

  NVstGF(sOprs6sWHptᶜd4rdrsN'mst mbl trmsRrptd ptᶜsHbn
nsrd n-Brptd njry. AprncWs c %(s mrkBV.ct w$Mdfn&tyrᶜZ
nft2B`rlrF&frEP.

  nrHWBnwᶜ,Ntn62R Brt) br(rn. WHwrnd (m frm tm2tmF
tmptsB(r lgs18r2xtc&nwrᶜ7jrsdk6VZ. WHrmndd (mF' os FR
mgr6&stl7hr. WHpld2(r n85jst9& 4nm8&WH"jUrd (mB'tIsFR
"n kndrd2dsvw (s Uspr6s w$ wd nvt7-ntrptR"x6s&"spndᶐs. Y
2HBn dEf2'voisFjst9&"sngn8. Wmst (r4aqscN'nss8w$ dnncsR
spr6&hld (mZWhld`rstFmnknd nmEsNwrNpEs frᶐs.

  W(r4`rprsᶜ85sF"Un@d st8sF AmrcaNgnrl"#smbld pl,2'sprm
jdgF" o 4`rct8FRntn6sDN'nm&B'(r8F"gdPF(s clns slm-pbl)&
dclrT(s Un@d ClnsR&Fr@Ot2BfrE&ndpndᶜst8s. TYRbslvd
frmLlgns2` Brt) crwn&TLpltkl"x6Btwn (m&' St8F Gr8 BrtnZ
&Ot2Bt@-dslvd&TZfrE&ndpndᶜst8sYH5pwr2lvy wr"cld pEs
"trct llncs stbl)"rs&DL(r cts&(,w$ ndpndᶐst8sMFr@D. &
4`sprtF(s dclr6W&frm rlnsN';tk6FDvn;vdnsWmUt-pldg2$(rR15
sRltns&Rscrd hnr.

When in the course of human events it becomes necessary for one people to dis-
solve the political bands which have connected them with another, and to assume,
among the powers of the earth, the separate and equal station to which the laws of
nature and Nature's God entitle them, a decent respect to the opinions of mankind
requires that they should declare the causes which impel them to the separation.

We hold these truths to be self-evident: That all men are created equal; that
they are endowed by their Creator with certain inalienable rights; that among these
are life, liberty, and the pursuit of happiness. That to secure these rights, governments are instituted among men, deriving their just powers from the consent of the
governed; that whenever any form of government becomes destructive of these ends,

it is the right of the people to alter or to abolish it, and to institute a new government, laying its foundation on such principles, and organizing its powers in such form as to them shall seem most likely to effect their safety and happiness. Prudence, indeed, will dictate that governments long established should not be changed for light and transient causes; and, accordingly, all experience hath shown that mankind are more disposed to suffer, while evils are sufferable, than to right themselves, by abolishing the forms to which they are accustomed. But when a long train of abuses and usurpations, pursuing invariably the same object, evinces a design to reduce them under absolute despotism, it is their right, their duty, to throw off such government, and to provide new guards for their future security. Such has been the patient sufferance of these colonies, and such is now the necessity which constrains them to alter their former systems of government. The history of the present king of Great Britain is a history of repeated injuries and usurpations, all having in direct object the establishment of an absolute tyranny over these States. To prove this, let facts be submitted to a candid world:

He has refused his assent to laws the most wholesome and necessary for the public good.

He has forbidden his governors to pass laws of immediate and pressing importance, unless suspended in their operation till his assent should be obtained; and when so suspended, he has utterly neglected to attend to them. He has refused to pass other laws for the accommodation of large districts of people, unless these people would relinquish the right of representation in the legislature—a right inestimable to them, and formidable to tyrants only.

He has called together legislative bodies at places unusual, uncomfortable, and distant from the repository of the public records, for the sole purpose of fatiguing them into complying with his measures.

He has dissolved representative houses repeatedly for opposing, with manly firmness, his invasions on the rights of the people.

He has refused for a long time after such dissolution, to cause others to be elected: whereby the legislative powers, incapable of annihilation, have returned to the people at large for their exercise, the state remaining, in the meantime, exposed to all the dangers of invasion from without and convulsions from within.

He has endeavored to prevent the population of these States: for that purpose obstructing the laws of naturalization of foreigners; refusing to pass others to encourage their migration hither, and raising the conditions of new appropriations of lands.

He has obstructed the administration of justice by refusing his assent to laws for establishing judiciary powers.

He has made judges dependent on his will alone for the tenure of their offices and the amount and payment of their salaries.

He has erected a multitude of new offices, and sent hither swarms of officers to harass our people and eat out their substance.

He has kept among us in times of peace, standing armies, without the consent of our legislatures.

He has effected to render the military independent of, and superior to, the civil power.

He has combined with others to subject us to a jurisdiction foreign to our Constitution, and unacknowledged by our laws; giving his assent to their pretended acts of legislation :

For quartering large bodies of armed troops among us :

For protecting them by a mock trial from punishment for any murders which they should commit on the inhabitants of these States :

For cutting off our trade with all parts of the world :

For imposing taxes on us without our consent :

For depriving us, in many cases, of the benefits of trial by jury :

For transporting us beyond seas to be tried for pretended offenses :

For abolishing the free system of English laws in a neighboring province, establishing therein an arbitrary government, and enlarging its boundaries, so as to render it at once an example and fit instrument for introducing the same absolute rule into these colonies :

For taking away our charters, abolishing our most valuable laws, and altering, fundamentally, the forms of our government :

For suspending our own legislatures, and declaring themselves invested with power to legislate for us in all cases whatsoever :

He has abdicated government here by declaring us out of his protection, and waging war against us :

He has plundered our seas, ravaged our coasts, burnt our towns, and destroyed the lives of our people :

He is at this time transporting large armies of foreign mercenaries to complete the works of death, desolation and tyranny already begun, with circumstances of cruelty and perfidy scarcely paralleled in the most barbarous ages, and totally unworthy the head of a civilized nation :

He has constrained our fellow-citizens, taken captive on the high seas, to bear arms against their country, to become the executioners of their friends and brethren, or to fall themselves by their hands :

He has excited domestic insurrections among us, and has endeavored to bring on the inhabitants of our frontiers, the merciless Indian savages, whose known rule of warfare is an undistinguished destruction of all ages, sexes and conditions.

In every stage of these oppressions we have petitioned for redress in the most humble terms; our repeated petitions have been answered only by repeated injury. A prince whose character is thus marked by every act which may define a tyrant is unfit to be the ruler of a free people.

Nor have we been wanting in attention to our British brethren. We have warned them, from time to time, of attempts by their legislature to extend an unwarrantable jurisdiction over us. We have reminded them of the circumstances of our emigration and settlement here. We have appealed to their native justice and magnanimity, and we have conjured them by the ties of our common kindred to disavow these usurpations, which would inevitably interrupt our connections and correspondence. They, too, have been deaf to the voice of justice and consanguinity. We must, therefore, acquiesce in the necessity which denounces our separation, and hold them, as we hold the rest of mankind, enemies in war, in peace, friends.

We, therefore, the representatives of the United States of America, in General Congress assembled, appealing to the Supreme Judge of the world for the rectitude of our intentions, do, in the name and by the authority of the good people of these colonies, solemnly publish and declare, that these United Colonies are, and of right ought to be, free and independent States; that they are absolved from all allegiance to the British Crown, and that all political connection between them and the State of Great Britain is, and ought to be, totally dissolved; and that, as free and independent states, they have full power to levy war, conclude peace, contract alliances, establish commerce and do all other acts and things which independent states may of right do. And for the support of this declaration, with a firm reliance on the protection of Divine Providence, we mutually pledge to each other our lives, our fortunes, and our sacred honor.

From " Hamlet."—Act III.

2BRnt2BTZ'qst6w(rTZnblrN'mnd2sfr's1, s&rOsFTrG:4tnR
2t/Ams gnst&CFtrbls&BOps, ɋ(m? 2D2s1pKmOr&B&s1p2CWnd'
hrt/&'(s&ntrl)ksTf1)ZAr2Z&"smt6dvt-2Bw)d. 2D2s1p 2s1p
pr$ns2drEm A(rZ'rb4NTs1pFd(wt drmsM"wnWH)f1dF(s mrtl coil
mst g5ZpAs. (rZ'rspctTm/s clm8FS1ng 15. 4Wwd bAr'whps
&scrnsFtIm'Oprsrs rng'prd mns"tUm-'pngsFdsprIzd lv'lws
dlA'nslnsFof9&'sprnsTp)ɋmrtF'nwr(Et/ wnHH6mIt hs qIAtus
m\W&bAr bdkn? Wwd (s frdls bAr2grnt&swtN&w315BT'drdF
sm(, /d('ndscvrd cnt3frmWs bOrnKtrvlr rtrns pzls'L&m/s

Żr(r bAr (sIlsWH(n f-2(rsTWKntF? (s"6s ds m∕cwrdsFZL&(s
'n85hUFrsl6Zskl EdOrW'pAl cstF(t& 3prlzsFgr8pt(&m07W(s
rgrd (r crçs trn wA&lUs'nAmFct6.

To be, or not to be, that is the question :
Whether 't is nobler in the mind, to suffer
The slings and arrows of outrageous fortune,
Or to take arms against a sea of troubles,
And, by opposing end them ?—To die,—to sleep,—
No more ; and, by a sleep, to say we end
The heart-ache, and the thousand natural shocks
That flesh is heir to,—'t is a consummation
Devoutly to be wish'd.   To die—to sleep ;—
To sleep ! perchance to dream ;—ay, there's the rub ;
For in that sleep of death what dreams may come,
When we have shuffled off this mortal coil,
Must give us pause : there 's the respect,
That makes calamity of so long life :
For who would bear the whips and scorns of time,
The oppressor's wrong, the proud man's contumely,
The pangs of dispriz'd love, the law's delay,
The insolence of office, and the spurns
 That patient merit of the unworthy takes,
When he himself might his quietus make
With a bare bodkin ?   Who would these fardels bear,
To grunt and sweat under a weary life ;
But that the dread of something after death,
The undiscovered country, from whose bourn
No traveller returns, puzzles the will ;
And makes us rather bear those ills we have,
Than fly to others that we know not of ?
Thus, conscience does make cowards of us all ;
And thus the native hue of resolution
Is sicklied o'er with the pale cast of thought ;
And enterprises of great pith and moment,
With this regard, their currents turn away,
And lose the name of action.

Form of Will.

'1s t LFM Jn JOnsF'twnF X4dN'cntyF Ok 1&&s t8F M$gnB, Fsnd
mIndT'tmFm⁄, &pb1), (sM1stL&tst7.

I g5&dv9LMstSrE1&prsn1 wrFIMDsEzdRpssd2 JAms BrwnF
'sd twnF X4d& Thms GrEnF'sm p192H&2h1d'sm2(m6s (r Ars&
asIns4VP'Uss&trsts flw, nm-

Ntrst frst2pALMdts&fnrl xpnss.

sknd2pA2Mw5 M3Phr sO1&spr8rsts'ntrstN'&rvnUFLMsd st8
dr, 'trmFhr n8r1 15.

&(rdP'dcEsFMsd w52'·vrtLMsd st8N2%Fs,$&crsSB(t bstBMsAd
trstEs&2pA2Mdtr Eln'&(rd_(rFTsm, 2Mbst2g5hrS1rg&)rNcntF
hr n782; vdlhr6&·rmn, 2(rds2BEq-dvddBtwnM4sns FrdrkStvn
Jms&JOn.

F(rFM$1drnSB4s$ dv6HdId 1v, 1w5)Us$)U2rsv'prᶜs)rBF(r
BK)U(n s$)r2f1N2'gnr1 fnd2Bdvdd mng'srvvrsN'mnrB4drktd.

&Ihr Bg52Msd trstEs5pwr&(r82s1&yRLFMrE1 st8Tprv8R
pb1ks1&nvst'; cdsR1Es'sm%YMdm bstl'ntrstFMfm-.

&FMdtr ElnSntHtnd'GFtwnty&P'dcsFhr m(rIhrBnmn8"st8
&pntMsd trsts grdnsF'prsn&st8FMsd dtr Eln dr,'rmndrFhr
mnr8"ᶜ, hr2(r f(r-cr&; tk8.

&IhrB"st8 Jms Brwn& ThmsGrEnMxk trsF(sM1stL&tst7.
NwtJwrFIHhrn2stMh&&s1 (s (rdDF Apr1N'yr1886.

JonJOns.

sInd sE1d pb1)d&dclrdB JonJOns'tst8r bv nmdZ&4hs 1st
L&tst7N'; snsFZWNhs; snsThs rqst&N'; snsF$ (rHhrn2stRnms
ZwtJs.

wtJs N. H.

wtJs F. S.

The last will of-me, John Jones, of-the-town of Oxford, in-the county of Oakland,
and State of Michigan, being of sound mind at-the-time of making and publishing this
my last will and testament.

37

I-give and devise all-my estate, real and personal, whereof I-may-die seized or possessed, to James Brown, of-the said town of Oxford, and Thomas Green, of-the-same place, to-have and-to-hold the-same to-themselves, their heirs and assigns forever, upon the-uses and trusts following, namely :

In-trust, first, to-pay all-my debts and funeral expenses.

Second, to-pay to-my wife, Mary, upon her sole and separate receipts, the-interest, income, and revenue of-all my said estate, during the-term of-her natural life.

And third, upon the-decease of my said wife, to convert all-my said estate into money, if such-a course shall-be thought best by my said trustees, and to-pay to-my daughter, Ellen, the one-third part thereof, it seeming to-me best to-give her so large a-share on-account-of her inability to provide for herself; and-the remaining two-thirds to-be equally divided between my four sons, Frederick, Stephen, James and John.

If either of-my children shall, before such division, have died, leaving lawful issue, such issue to-receive the-parent's share, but, if-there-be no issue, then such share to-fall into-the general fund, to-be divided among the-survivors in-the manner before directed.

And L-hereby give to-my said trustees full power and authority to-sell any or all of-my real estate at private or public sale, and invest the proceeds, or lease the-same, as they-may deem best for-the interest of-my family.

And if my daughter Ellen shall-not-have attained the age of twenty-one upon-the decease of-her mother, I-hereby nominate, constitute, and appoint my said trustees guardians of-the person and estate of-my said daughter, Ellen, during the-remainder of-her minority, commending her to-their fatherly care and protection.

And I-hereby constitute James Brown and Thomas Green my executors of-this my last will and testament.

In-witness whereof, I-have hereunto set my hand and seal, this third day of April, in-the year 1886.   JOHN JONES.

Signed, sealed, published, and declared by John Jones, the testator above named, as and-for his last will and testament, in-the presence, of us, who, in-his presence, at-his request, and-in-the presence of-each other, have hereunto set-our names as witnesses.

Witnesses : N. H.
          F. S.

Partnership Agreement.

(s gr7m8(s ff(DFAgst1886BtwnThmsH. Sm(F Chrlstn S. C. F'&_& ChrlsT. ClnF'sm p19F'(r_wtJ(.

'sd_Es grE2ssOC8(m6Zco_nrs4&prdF5yrs f'm (sd8N'bsJFbI,&

sl, hrdwr&s$ (r gds&"d8sZblngNTlInF'trd'nm&stllF'frm2B
Sm(&Culn.

4'prpsF"dct,'bsJF'bv nmd_nrJ ThmsH. Sm(hsT'd8F(s r@,
nvstd5000$ Zcptl stk&'sd ChrlsT.Culn hs pdN'l/smF5000$ b(
Fw$ mntsR2Bxpéd&UsdN"n4'mtl dvntGF'_s hr2N'mnG7F(r bsJ.

TZhrBLSgrEdBb(_Es hr2TYLnt wl ss8dZco_nrs flO&y
vk6Rtrd2(rOn prv8dvntGBL(rT'ntr prdFco nrJpt4((r tmst&bst
54ts4(r mtl dvntG&'ncrsF'cptl stk.

T'dtlsF'bsJMB(r-NstdB$TZgrdTdr,'4sd prd cr8&5bk cntsS
Bkpt wrN$_nrSrcrdRcaus2Bntrd&rcrdd5mn6FL %rsvd&xpédZ
wlZVrtcl pr$sd&sld blng,2RN&ywIs prtn,2s$_nrJ'gns;fts
xpédtrs&lssB,Eq-dv@dBtwn (m. TZfr(r grdT&cVyrRfnr)d
(r_y dsr&5jst&cr8xbtSBmS2$(rR2(r xctrsRdmnst8rsRrpsé85s
F'lss rsEts;fts&ncrs m8BrsnFRrs,frms$ co_nrJ. &/s$ xbt
Zm8'srpls;ftFs$ (rBrslt,frm'bzJSBdv@dBtwn'sbscrb,_s)r&
)rl/.

E(r_y hr2SBlwd2drw&sm nt xd,600$pr anum frm'cptl
stkF'frmNmn(-nstl7sF50$$w$ mntMBncrsdBsbsqégr7.

&fr(r)d (r_y dsrR)d d(F(r_sR(r rsns m/Tnss3Y'sd co_nrs
L$2'(rRNcAsFd(F(r'srvv,_y2'xktrsRdmnstr8rsF'_y dcsd m/&5
cr8&fnl cntF"d6F'_nrJZ/sd&Lfr-&cr8-ajst'sm. &LSPtk,&
nvé3Fsd cptl stkWncrs&;ft (rNw$SprRZfnd2Brmn,Ls$ rmndrSB
Eq-pr)6d&dv@dBtwn (m'sd co_nrs (r xctrsRdmmstr8rs)r&)rl/.

TZLSgrdTNcsF&msNst&,rs,W'_nrs hr2w$ céBstldBtwn (m6s
s$ dfrnsFpn6sBstldBrbtS6P'flw,"d6s2wt$_y2SUs&rbtSr wS2(s
lctdS$Us&(rd'3(s $sn2dtrmn'mrtsF'cs&rng'bsisF&stl7.

NwtJwrF'Nsnd hr2st (r h&s'D&yr frst bv r@n.

ThmsH. Sm(.
Chs. T. Culn.

sIndN';snsF

D. L. Silrs.
E. A. Kendy.

This agreement, made this fifth day of August, 1886, between Thomas H. Smith, of Charleston, S. C., of-the one part, and Charles T. Cullen, of-the-same place, of-the other part, witnesseth:

The-said parties agree to-associate themselves as copartners, for-a period of five years from-this date, in-the business of buying and selling hardware and-such other goods and commodities as belong in-that line of trade; the-name and style of-the firm to-be Smith & Cullen.

For-the purpose of conducting the-business of-the above named partnership, Thomas H. Smith, has, at-the-date of-this writing, invested Five Thousand Dollars as capital stock, and-the said Charles T. Cullen has paid in the-like sum of Five Thousand Dollars, both of-which amounts are to-be expended and used in common for-the mutual advantage of-the parties hereto in-the management of-their business.

It-is hereby also agreed by both parties hereto, that-they-will-not, while associated as copartners, follow any avocation or trade to-their-own private advantage, but-will, throughout the-entire period of-copartnership, put-forth-their utmost and-best efforts for-their mutual advantage and-the increase of-the capital stock.   •

That-the details of-the business may-be thoroughly understood by each, it-is agreed that, during the aforesaid period, accurate and-full book accounts shall-be kept, where-in each partner shall record, or caused to-be entered and recorded, full mention of-all money received and expended, as-well as every article purchased and sold belonging to, or in anywise appertaining to-such partnership; the-gains, profits, expenditures and losses being equally divided between them. It is further agreed that once every year, or oftener, should either party desire, a-full, just and accurate exhibit shall-be made to-each other, or to their executors, administrators or representatives, of-the loses, receipts, profits and increase made by reason of, or arising from, such copartnership. And, after such exhibit is made, the surplus profit, if, such there-be, resulting from-the business, shall-be divided between the subscribing partners, share and share alike.

Either party hereto shall be allowed to-draw a-sum, not exceeding six hundred dollars per-annum, from the capital stock of-the firm, in monthly installments of fifty dollars each, which amount may-be increased by subsequent agreement.

And further, should either party desire, or should death of either of-the parties, or other reasons, make it necessary, they, the-said copartners, will each to-the other, or, in-case of death of-either, the surviving party to-the executors or administrators of-the party deceased, make a-full, accurate and final account of-the condition of-the partner-ship as aforesaid, and-will fairly and accurately adjust the-same. And also, upon taking an inventory of-said capital stock, with increase and profit thereon, which-shall appear or is found to be remaining, all-such remainder shall-be equally apportioned and divided between-them, the-said copartners, their executors or administrators, share and share alike.

It-is also agreed, that in-case of-a misunderstanding arising with the partners here-to, which-cannot-be settled between themselves, such differences of opinion shall-be settled by arbitration, upon the-following conditions, to-wit: Each party to-choose one arbitrator, which two thus elected shall choose a third ; the three thus chosen to-determine the-merits of-the case, and arrange the-basis of-a settlement.

In witness whereof, the undersigned hereto set-their hands, the-day and year first above written.

THOMAS H. SMITH.
CHARLES T. CULLEN.

Signed in presence of
  D. L. SILLERS.
  E. A. KENNEDY.

— — —

Form of Lease.

(s grE7RlEs m8(s (rdDF Aprl BtwnAbnrSm(F GrEnfld O. _yF'frst_& Chas. DnlsF DErbrnO. _yF'scnd_wtJ(.

T'sd_yF'frst_dsB(s;scs lEs 2'sd_yF'scnd_'flw, dscrbd ;rt.y2wt. dscrb;prty.

2H&2hld'sm2'sd _yF'scnd_frm'5(DF Aprl 1886 2'5(DF Aprl 1887.

&'sd_yF'scnd_cvnes&grEsW'_yF'frst_2pA'sd_yF'frst_Z rç4'sm'smF800$p7Zflws2wt. st8'tm&trmsFpA7.

'sd_yF'scnd_fr(r cvnesW'sd_yF'frst_TT'xpr6F'tIm mn6dN(s lEs pc7pss6F'sd;mssSBg5n2'sd_yF'frst_NZgd''d6ZYnwR'U)lwAr nv@7cdçs lsBfr xptd&TP'nonp7F'wOlR&ypr6F'sd rçT'tm wn'sm Z;msd2Bpd'sd_yF'frst. MThs lc6E(r dstrn4sd rçdURdclr (s lEsT&nd&rcvr pss6F'sd;mssZF'sm wr hldB4s7dtnr'sd_yF'scnd_ wv, &y ntcFs$ lc6R&y dm&4'pss6F'sd;mss.

'cvnes hrNSxtç2&Bbnd, P'hrs xctrs&dmnstr8rsF'_s2(s lEs. wtJsd_s h&s&SEls.

sgn8rF lessor.
sgn8rF lessee.

45

This agreement or lease, made this third day of April, between Abner Smith, of Greenfield, Ohio. party of the first part, and Chas. Daniels, of Dearborn, Ohio, party of the second part, witnesseth :

That the said party of the first part does by these presents lease to the said party of the second part the following described property, to-wit :   [Describe property.]

To have and to hold the same to the said party of the second part, from the fifth day of April, 1886, to the fifth day of April, 1887.

And the said party of the second part covenants and agrees with the party of the first part to pay the said party of the first part, as rent for the same, the sum of $800, payable as follows, to-wit :   [State the times and terms of payment.]

The said party of the second part further covenants with the said party of the first part, that, at the expiration of the time mentioned in this lease, peaceable possession of the said premises shall be given to the said party of the first part, in as good condition as they now are, the usual wear, inevitable accidents, loss by fire excepted ; and that upon the non-payment of the whole or any portion of the said rent at the time when the same is promised to be paid, the said party of the first part may, at his election, either dis-train for said rent due, or declare this lease at an end, and recover possession of said premises as if the same were held by forcible detainer, the said party of the second part waiving any notice of such election, or any demand for the possession of said premises.

The covenants herein shall extend to and be binding upon the heirs, executors and administrators of the parties to this lease.

Witness said parties' hands and seals.

(Signature of Lessor.)   [SEAL.]
(Signature of Lessee.)   [SEAL]

Shorthand and Typewriting. - *N. Y. Daily.*

'1st fw DsHBn mpr t&&sN'hst3F')r t&4YwtJd'd(F AndrwJ. GrahmT OrngN. J. &'"'fr, F'rdrFnI tQBQ VctraP Isaac Ptmn.

Ptmn WⅩnw pst 80yrsFGⅩ'f(rF' mdrn rtFvrbtm rprt, & GrhmWptT&sstmFhs On bsdP PtmnsW&F'frst2pret9'rtN Amrc.

Ptmns nvc6W'rs1 tF&$ngFrlg:fA(Nhs_.   N1835 wnHW22yrs 1dHW&t$rN& Engl) skl"dctdN'sp9sF'$F Engl&.   'r@ ,sF Swdn brg flN2hs&s& PtmnBcm&'"vr t2'dctrn st4(N (m,   (s nss t8d hs g5, Phs st6 'w$Hpnd&sk1N B(.   Htrnd hs tn62spl, rfrmNv¢, frst&1fbt''tn, & c 4VsndBVsmlrNpr¢c2'"n Rmn 1fbt.   (nHw¢&stp

fr(r&fOngrfc)rt&W'rslt.　TZ;pb7-nt srt, 2m$2CTR Ptmns
nv&6Z&F'tnRtwlv mst bnf)lF'ntr &3.　Ths"plt-rvl6Izd rprt,
&ltr wrt,.

　jst hw m&y)rt&r@trs (rRNnU YrkTwdBdfclt2st8;pb7-
frm4500tU5000.　'#hs ncrsdWgr8rpd8dr, 'lst3R4yrs&(rRnw
;b7-mr wmn (n mnNnU YrkWm⁄(r lv, N(s wA.　N1887(r wr bt
2500)rt&r@rs hrLtldFwm bt1000wr wmn.　'frst wmn2r@)rt&
hrW&Rs Stfrd.　Sbgn hr wrk bt25yrsG.　prIr2TtmTWhldTwmn
cd nt r@)rt&.　hr scs hvrWSmrkdZ2m⁄hr fm:&2ndUs lrg #s
F (r wmn2flONhr ft stps.　'frst mn2r@)rt&hrW d Houstn&
nwsppr rprtr.　Hbgn bt 45yrsG.　' 3dc6F"tpr@, m)Ens gv
)rt&r@, Ts gr8bUm.

　'pAF)rt&r@rs sd&xprt rprtr2'r@r ystrDZnt wtTUsd2B'tr(
b, qItZgr8-xgr8d ftntms·crn, TZrgrd, spEd.　Of)l crt rprtrs
NnU Yrk gt frm2000tU3000$&yr.　)rt&clrks gtL'wAfrm8$4w$
m&y r(r nxprt yng grls wrkPto 25S&35$B(sWrcv'ltr fgrR
VfUN#.　bsJ)rt&r@rsDnt nd ftn2r@mr (n60R80wrds&mn@&wn
Yr@fstrTZB4&fUmn@sT&tm.　VfUr@rsKsstnl50wrds&mn@&'tlk
Fr@, 250 wrdsZrnk nnsns.　mstF'bg strEsFfnmnl)rt&fEts
cm frm'fr Wst.　'fr(r wAfrm nU Yrk'srcF'st3'hIr'r8.　nt lng
G(rW&yrn bt&mnWWmbt: 2r@300wrds&mn@.　Hprct9dWsd8B
D'Vbst HcdHcdn-r$297.　TW&gd st3TWwl tld&T 3std svrlF
ZmIt-.　(r4Wtk pns2rnTdwn&fndTTcm frm Clf4na.　IHtstdMOn
spd sd (s)rt&r@r&fndTwn fl, wllKDbt165wrds4&"sdr7lng(F
tIm.　I(nk IM&gd mn&IKT&mnWKvrG175wrds&mn@4&hrZfrst cls.
(rMB&dznRfftEnN(s twnWKDT&prps (rR40R50WKD150wrds&mn@
L(OVm&y wmnHcmN2'bsJ&Rqt cpt74bsJwrk&4vr: (r4msFdct86yt
wnTcms2lng strn, wrk l⁄cOrt wrk&rprt, lng sp$sYHnt'fskl
strn(.　I)dCTTwd t⁄bt2yrs4&prsnWZwl ftdZ2tmpr7&strctrF
'h&s2B·&xprt r@rF)rt&.　wn&yng mnWhs prctsd5R6mn(s
tlsMHKDfrm 125tU130wrds&mn@I·cldTHKr-gt wAWbt60R75&
xprns hs)OnTM·cl6ZU)-r@.

The last few days have been important ones in the history of shorthand, for they witnessed the death of Andrew J. Graham at Orange, N. J., and the conferring of the order of knighthood by Queen Victoria upon Isaac Pittman.

Pittman, who is now past 80 years of age, is the father of the modern art of verbatim reporting, and Graham, who put out a system of his own, based upon Pittman's, was one of the first to practice the art in America.

Pittman's invention was the result of a change of religious faith on his part. In 1835, when he was 22 years old, he was a teacher in an English school conducted under the auspices of the Church of England. The writings of Swedenborg fell into his hands, and Pittman became a convert to the doctrines set forth in them. This necessitated his giving up his situation, after which he opened a school in Bath. He turned his attention to spelling reform, inventing first an alphabet containing a character for every sound, but very similar in appearance to the common Roman alphabet. Then he went a step further and phonographic shorthand was the result. It is probably not asserting too much to say that Mr. Pittman's invention is one of the ten or twelve most beneficial of the entire century. It has completely revolutionized reporting and letter writing.

Just how many shorthand writers there are in New York it would be difficult to state, probably from 4500 to 5000. The number has increased with great rapidity during the last three or four years, and there are now probably more women than men in New York, who make their living in this way. In 1887 there were about 2500 shorthand writers here all told, of whom about 1000 were women. The first woman to write shorthand here was a Mrs. Stafford. She began her work about twenty-five years ago. Prior to that time it was held that women could not write shorthand. Her success, however, was so marked as to make her famous and induce large numbers of other women to follow in her footsteps. The first man to write shorthand here was Dr. Houston, a newspaper reporter. He began about forty-five years ago. The introduction of the typewriting machines gave shorthand writing its great boom.

" The pay of shorthand writers?" said an expert reporter to the writer yesterday, " is not what it used to be, the truth being quite as greatly exaggerated oftentimes concerning it as regarding speed. Official court reporters in New York get from $2000 to $3000 a year. Shorthand clerks get all the way from $8, for which many rather inexpert young girls work, up to $25 and $35, but those who receive the latter figure are very few in number. Business shorthand writers do not need often to write more than sixty or eighty words a minute, and when they write faster, it is but for a few minutes at a time. Very few writers can sustain 150 words a minute, and the talk of writing 250 words is rank nonsense. Most of the big stories of phenomenal shorthand feats come from the far West. The further away from New York the source of the story the higher the rate. Not long ago there was a yarn about a man who was ambitious to write 300 words a minute. He practiced with assiduity, but do the very best he could, he could only reach 297. It was a good story, it was well told, and it interested several of us mightily. Therefore we took pains to run it down, and found that it came from California. " I have tested my own speed," said this shorthand writer, " and find that when feeling well I can do about 165 words for a considerable length of time. I think I am a good man, and I know that a man who can average 175 words a minute for an hour is first-class. There may be a dozen or fifteen in this town who can do that, and perhaps there are forty or fifty who can do 150 words a minute. Although very many women have come into the business and are quite acceptable for business work, and for various other forms of dictation, yet when it comes to long straining work like court work and reporting long speeches, they have not the physical strength. I should say that it would take about two years for a person who is well fitted as to temperament and structure of the hands to become an expert writer of shorthand. When a young man who has practiced five or six months tells me he can do from 125 to 130 words a minute I conclude that he can really get away with about sixty or seventy-five, and experience has shown that my conclusion is usually right."

"clUd, rmks. †

N"clUd, (s ltl trt9'A(r bgs2st8&$1ngs&y rprtrN Amrca 2gAnChs rmrksTwrV&tIpr@, m)EnKBUsd stn@pEsrpssNspEd& 1gb18VKn sstmF)rt&. NdEdL4msFmnl)rt& mstNvt7-B"obs18. 'tr-ds nt mr xl'ld bZRbb tAl hrs cr (n stn@pE'mprt.k7&rd: sstmFfOnO&stngrfE. TLmst trbls'spEdFrdn3tIpr@, wlst rd, xrc9sO, 2'frqncyFcptlsRmr 1g7(n"n bUk prnt. 2¡v (s n-& wEks stdEF'sstm%nss3. N'4G, xrc9s'rEdr vn (OnqntdW)rt& KCT&&cTTrqrs&-#FmO6F'&2r@&frAsBs tn@pE(n2xprs'sAm/Ptmn GrhmPrnnMnsn McKE&s$ nv&trs. r@, T&spEdF150wrds&mn@K Umn h&K¡pr-bsrv2ps6s bv2B1C&&N'1InZ McKENhs nU Rpd t$s wlst')Ad, '1Ups&hks&h1f5&db1 1InsF Ptmns sstm&(s bAsdPT rndr"ct r@, &fcE1 rd, LBmps7. T%LSwr(yFnt9TNstn@pE (rR fUr grmlgs&brv86sTBmmr9d. 2pGsF' 1fbt mbr9'ntIr sstm. L'xrc9sN'¡s&wrkKBrdB&rdn3std&N-(n2wEks. L'A(r sksF&Kdd

† NOTE:—Although great care has been devoted to the proof-reading, still it is to be feared that some errors have been over-looked in a work so complex.

pb1kZTg5'wrk&fAr trI1 pA, Ktn62dvrt97s w$Nnmr:Nst¢sR1dt3
R"dmnt3crd, 2'mnt xp¢dd. Fstn@pEhdK(r dv¢GBTFB, &tIm sAvr
2tIp st, mSEns&rd, m8Esy2dtrs lwyrs&clrgmn'nv¢6wldB&wl"
sst¢. +dct86&vrbtm rprt, stn@pE nh&cs'mrtsF'tIpr@r&m/s
fst r@, &"ct rEd, &pls¢xrc9.

n1/mst (rt&mnlsTmr-g5lsns dptd2$ p $ptrFrUls&xcp8s
'prs¢wrk g5s&vArEd slc6ncld, wrds&frAssTRstmb1, blks2L
rprtrs. L'xrc9sRrtnNwt rprtrs cLrprt, WTwst, tImB'Scld
"spnd, stI1.

Z'Ar cstlsFU(5mb6Rgrdl-dspEr, 'A(r nwN'Evn, Fhs dcl, yrs
avrsT+Kr (-"sdr6cdHBndUcd2fr&wr (-Rsprf)1 dv92&Nt1G¢
Engl) spk, P. mrV Engl) spk, PRnt Es-mpsdP. h¢F&y&"s
4_&; vsTwtZclAmdN'tItl pGF(s bUk1tZgrnd-smp6'A(rLBmn g'frst
2"sIn stn@pE2wOlsAl crEm6. TwdLmstB&mrcl2HskUls&clGs
_W(r rmnr85pt sstms4smtIm2". B4stn@pEB"&1tr3&fn&)1 scs
&1tl rsrvd pA)csLBnss3. Bxhst5lbr&frtl brAnsRv¢-)Ur 2
pr)8&sstm w$ rlvs'std¢frm hvy&1@ strks&frEsHfrm hks&lps.
O1 jmp, JckN'bx nw bv nwB1O&gn P'1InZ5-mnsp8d. HnEdsB
tp'kEs&stn@pELD'rst.

Concluding Remarks.

In concluding this little treatise, the author begs to state and challenges any reporter
in America to gainsay his remarks, that wherever a typewriting machine can be
used, Stenotypy surpasses in speed and legibility, every known system of shorthand.
Indeed, all forms of *manual* shorthand must inevitably become obsolete. The trolley
does not more excel the old " buss," or bob-tail horse-car, than Stenotypy the impracti-
cable and arduous systems of phonography and stenography. It almost trebles the
speed of ordinary typewriting; whilst reading exercises, owing to the frequency of
capitals, are more legible than common book-print. To prove this only one week's
study of the system is necessary. In the foregoing exercises, the reader, even though
unacquainted with shorthand, can see at once, that it requires a less number of motions
of the hand to write a phrase by Stenotypy than to express the same after Pitman, Graham, Pernin, Munson, McKee and such inventors. Writing at a speed of 150 words a
minute, no human hand can properly observe *two* positions *above*, *two below*, and *one*
on the line, as McKee, in his " New Rapid " teaches, whilst the shading, the loops

and hoops and half full and double lines of Pitman's system and those based upon it, render correct writing and facile reading all but impossible. It is also worthy of notice that in Stenotype there are fewer grammalogues and abbreviations to be memorized. Two pages of the alphabet embrace the entire system. All the exercises in the present work can be read by an ordinary student in less than two weeks. All the Author asks of a candid Public is to give the work a fair trial, paying no attention to advertisements which, in numerous instances, are laudatory or condemnatory, according to the amount expended.

If Stenotype had no other advantage but that of being a time-saver to type-setting machines, a "reading-made-easy" to Editors, Lawyers and Clergymen, the invention would be a welcome assistant. For dictation and verbatim reporting, Stenotype enhances the merits of the typewriter, and makes fast writing and correct reading a pleasant exercise.

Unlike most shorthand manuals that merely give lessons adapted to each *particular chapter* of rules and exceptions, the present work gives a varied selection, including words and phrases that are stumbling blocks to all reporters. All the exercises are written in what reporters call the "reporting," without wasting time by the so-called corresponding style.

As the air-castles of youthful ambition are gradually disappearing, the Author, now in the evening of his declining years, avers that for no earthly consideration could he be induced to offer a worthless or superficial device to an intelligent English-speaking people. Moreover, English-speaking people are not easily imposed upon. Hence, if any one comes forward and proves that what is claimed in the title page of this booklet is groundless assumption, the Author will be among the first to consign Stenotype to wholesale cremation. It would almost be a miracle to have schools and colleges part with their remunerative pet systems for some time to come. Before Stenotype becomes a literary and financial success, a little reserved patience will be necessary. But exhaustive labor and fertile brains are eventually sure to appreciate a system which relieves the student from *heavy* and light strokes and frees him from hooks and loops. Old Jumping Jack-in-the-box, now *above*, now *below*, and again *upon* the line, is fully emancipated. He needs but tap the keys and Stenotypy will do the rest.

D. A. Q.

NOTE:—In preparing this edition the Author is pleased to acknowledge valuable suggestions by the Bishop of Denver, Right Rev. N. Matz, D. D.

A Concise Explanation

A typewriter who can write 60 words a minute can, by using the logograms of Stenotypy, multiply this rate by two and a half (*at least*), speeding 150 words a minute, or *saving* of *six* out of *ten* hours' labor. Eighty words a minute (a speed which hundreds of typewriters attain), would, by Stenotypy, average 200 words per minute – a speed which no living reporter, who writes legibly, can ever reach by any other system. The Stenotyper writes in this rapid way *every word*, using vowels and consonants that in no other system could be used. This is not a gratuitous assumption, but an *evidence* which the preceding exercises *visibly* demonstrate. The word-signs are so suggestive and plain, that in less than five years the Author expects to see bibles, hymnals and prayer-books in the hands of the " old folk," who have discarded their spectacles since this CAPITAL system came into use. There can be no possible confusion in regard to word-spacing. In fact the collocation of capital letters and other logograms, without space, is a beautiful feature of the art. We will explain:

" All the consonants of the English alphabet, when written as CAPITALS, are *logograms* or *word-signs* that require no *space* before or after. Four letters, G J Q X , (being of less frequent use), are also used for *affixes* besides being word-signs. The capital letter B invariably stands for *be, by, but*; C stands for *say, sea, see*. It can never mean anything else. D is used to express *day, die, do;* F is the word-sign for *of, if. off*; G stands for *God, go, age*. It is used for *age* wherever these three letters occur, whether used in the beginning or end of a word, as G¢.(agent) ; mrG (marriage). The *capital* vowels, like *capital* consonants, have no space *before* or *after* them. I O U always stand for the words they phonetically express. OURMfr¢ (Oh! You are my friend), is more legible than the sentence spelt out in full. In like manner, the figures are used for the words they phonetically express. The figure 2 stands for *to, too, two*; 4 is a word-sign, meaning *for*, *fore, four*, as in 4G, (foregoing). The figures 8 and 9 follow the same rule. p8 (pate) ; q1g (quinine), whilst they, in common with the other figures and punctuation marks, stand for the *affixes* placed opposite them in the alphabet or key. If there is no space *before* or *after* the the figure or stop, you know it is used for an *affix*. cp7F (capable of). Here, the figure 7 (meaning able, ment), having no space to left or right, is used as an *affix*. When used as a *prefix*, it must have one space to left. TZV 7vEnC (It is very inconvenient). The figure 7 as a *prefix*, stands for *incom-n, incog, encoun*. The commercial C besides standing for *cent-s*, also stands for ant, ent. Where a word-sign is used in the middle of a word, as "&7 (commandment) ; 4_J (forwardness). The & and _ being used for *and-ward*, there can be no mistaking the meaning. The J here would also mean Jesus or Jew, but the context will readily show the correct meaning. In regard to word-spacing, the guiding rules may all be expressed in one sentence, viz :—Wherever a CAPITAL letter, figure, or stop is used for a *word-sign*, there will be no space *before* or *after* such capital letter, figure, or stop. Each word-sign always retains its meaning as given in the alphabet."

The student will find the reading of Stenotypy so easy, that the rules for *spacing* between words that end with a *small* vowel or consonant, might in numerous instances, be overlooked. The word-signs are so frequently used that they assist the reader whenever the writer failed to observe the rules of word-spacing.

In concluding this little volume, the Author expresses sorrow for having so unsparingly to disparage other shorthand systems, but the wearisome defects of these systems were so apparent and numerous that no honest instructor could overlook them.

Whilst the human eye is undimmed, and the intellect capable of discerning metaphysical and physical excellence, there can be no hesitation in choosing a system which requires but a gentle tap with any of the ten fingers to form a syllable or word, in preference to those *pen* and *pencil* systems that require *three* positions, (McKee has *five*) *above, below* and *on* the line of *horizontal, oblique* or *vertical* strokes which must (in Pitmanic systems), be in *heavy* or *light* shading, and of *half, whole* or *double length*. The hooks, loops, circles, dots and other technical devices, used to express word-combinations or vowels are as puzzling as the hieroglyphics on a Chinese tea-chest. Hence no reporter would attempt to read the writing of another. Indeed, every first-class reporter must candidly admit, that while keeping pace with the human voice he must often depend on his memory and his own creations. The fact that Stenotypy exercises can be read at sight by anyone who knows the key or alphabet, must be regarded as a most valuable feature. In the words of the learned Bishop of Denver, 4lg7S&spEstn@pExlsV Kn sstmF)rt&. (" For *legibility* and *speed*, Stenotypy excels every known system of shorthand.")

19

APPENDIX.

The following list of words, besides being a pleasant exercise, affords an ocular evidence of the brevity of Stenotype. No system of shorthand is capable of such contractions. It will be seen that besides *prefixes and affixes*, contractions are used in the middle of words. Although the same word-signs (such as T for "that," "it" and "out") are used, still there will be no doubt about which word is meant in the sentence, as the context will always indicate the proper word.

B4&	beforehand.	ts t%	testimony.
dv¢G	advantage.	pA(¢	patient.
Ny (,	anything.	rdn3	ordinary.
a__7	apartment.	; v8	private.
"__7	compartment.	; d¢	prudent.
4 t8	fortitude.	; v¢6	prevention.
Urs f(5-NX { yours faithfully in Christ.		; ts t¢	protestant.
4 tU8	fortuity.	c	catholic.
xc@	execute.	s cr f9	sacrifice.
xc@5	executive.	s cr7	sacrament.
ddc83	dedicatory.	;vdnc	Providence.
4 g5J	forgiveness.	pl¢A6s	plantations.
1w-J	lawlessness.	grAc:	gracious.
M6	myself.	n.__J	inwardness.
H6	himself.	Nt/,	undertaking.
6)J	selfishness.	T15	outlive.
2@	contrite.	15-Q	livelihood.

2m&	countermand.	w¢,	wanting.
3dc6	introduction.	LJ	lordship.
4fs¢	magnificent.	lUn9	lunacy.
5mT	transmit.	;mOt or ;m@	promote.
6t7	accountable.	;vId or ;v@	provide.
6t&̧	accountant.	.;#	progress.
7plEt	incomplete.	;jd9	prejudice.
8t	recount.	;prA6	preparation.
9#6	retrogression.	rlA6	relation.
2vrsy	controversy.	rIt& or r@&	righthand.
TrG:	outrageous.	fcEt:	facetious.
T#	outnumber.	ndc8	indicate.
""t&̧	concomitant.	nv&̧6	invention.
"c9	concise.	n8	innate.
"pr85	comparative.	mdE8	mediate.
"pr6	comparison.	md8-	immediately.
"4m8	conformity.	mdt8	meditate.
w/5	wakeful.	ntxc8	intoxicate.
5#6	transgression.	jnU3	January.
6p&y	accompany.	snD	Sunday.
2dct3	contradictory.	wrF	whereof.
t&̧5	attentive.	wr4	wherefore.
"sE&̧:	conscientious.	fmn9	feminine.
vOt5	votive.	hIl&	highland.
#-	numberless.	mpr85	imperative.
"#	congress.	mprt&̧	impertinent.
cOpr8	co-operate.	clt58	cultivate.
"5	connive.	(,	thing.

It must be noticed that the above list of words are almost all spelt out in full. Trangression (5#6). The 5 with space to left is prefix for *trans;* # is affix for *gress;* 6 is affix for *sion.* A glance at the alphabet will show what each character means.

51

CORRIGENDA.

Page 7, fourth line from bottom tOm (tone), should be tOn.

The sign % which is used as an affix for (*ony-mony*), and for the prefix *circum*, is also used for the prefixes (*sub-sur*), which we have failed to insert in the alphabet on page 9.

The inverted commas (") which stand for the prefixes (*com-con-cor*) is also used for the prefix (*col*). Omitted on page 9.

Page 9, cm&7 (commandment), should be "&7.

Page 10, in the context, that sentence commencing " *Grammalogues that take s to form their plurals, etc.*," should read " *Logograms that take s to form their plurals, etc.*"

Page 20, fourth line from top, W& (wand), should be w&.

Page 22, first line, cn (can), should be K.

Page 23, insert $ between six and seventh letter from end of line five.

Page 24, fourth line from bottom, WEZ (with ease), should be WEz.

Page 29, third last word of line one, n@A6 (invitation), should be nv@6.

Page 30, fourth line of " Declaration of Independence;" change 2'stl6 (to the separation), to 2'sprA6.

Page 30, third line from bottom of page, the first four words should read lgslSr&r@ nstm72.

Page 39, line seven, co nrJ (copartnership), should be co__nrJ.

Until the student has attained sufficient proficiency in Stenotypy the numerical *prefixes* given in the alphabet (page 9), being seldom used might be omitted. *Word-spacing*, which has been invariable observed between *small consonant* letters that belong to different words, might also be discarded, after a time, as logograms, or word-signs are sufficiently numerous to prevent confusion in the reading of exercises.

TESTIMONIALS.

The reader must bear in mind that Stenotypy, being *recently* invented (important additions having been made as late as March 1st, 1895), the system, therefore, lacked the time necessary to submit it to a candid public criticism. Moreover, few shorthand experts are capable of giving a fair opinion as to its merits. In a letter which we herein publish from the " Caligraph Co.," it will also be seen how Stenotypy is handicapped by the red tape used in our colleges and schools where phonographic *manual* systems are taught.

The few letters we subjoin, coming from persons whose probity and scholarly attainments are beyond question, *recommend* more than columns of paid advertisements.

Bishop's House, 235 S. Evans Street,

Denver, Col., Dec. 9, 1894.

Rev. D. A. Quinn :—

Rev. and Dear Father—Your very kind letter and the books you so kindly sent me came to hand. As you will see, I have already become somewhat familiar with your system of Stenotypy. Whatever the hypocritical may think about it, I am satisfied that it meets a long felt want. I have often been wondering that someone did not invent long ago some system of shorthand for the typewriter. You have solved the problem. Perhaps some one will say it is not philosophical, as Mr. Pittman claims for his phonography. No matter, if it does the work. I fear some one will claim and try to wrest from you the glory of giving us a new invention of great value. At all events I consider you an inventor, and as such, I, for one, shall ever be most grateful to you. This is the second letter I write according to your system. The more I practice it, the better I like it. I have written to Father G—, of Santa Fe., recommending it and urging its adoption in the schools. Like every good thing it demands patience and practice. But the person who has the courage to bestow these will be amply rewarded. Now, my dear Father Quinn, let me again thank you for sending me this work of yours. I assure you I am deeply grateful to you for it and I shall never sit down to my machine to write by this system without thinking of you, and learning every day more and more to appreciate the boon you have conferred on humanity by your system of stenotypy.

Very sincerely yours in Xt.,

N. C. MATZ,

Bishop of Denver.

53

The Bishop found the system so simple that he wrote the above letter in Stenotypy (almost without a mistake) after less than one week's practice.

In a letter dated February 5, 1895, the Bishop wrote: "For *legibility* and *rapidity* your system is infinitely preferable to any of the known systems of shorthand. The fact that in two days I got control of its principles, shows how easy of acquisition and practical your invention is. For those who have neither the time nor aptitude to learn any of the complicated systems in vogue, Stenotypy is invaluable."

NOTE:—McKee, in his introduction to his "New Rapid ' Shorthand, proves that Pitman's boasted claim to philosophy and nature is a false allegation. McKee clearly shows that most of the Pitmanic loops, hooks and vowels are used in direct *contradiction* to his (Pitman's) principles. The author of Stenotypy, however, fails to see where Mr. McKee has given a better substitute for Pittman's combinations. McKee's *quintuple* vowel system, as also his half, whole and double length strokes, although aiding speed, will forever remain an insurmountable obstacle to *legibility*, which, in all cases, is more necessary than any rate of speed.

CHANCELLOR'S OFFICE,

DIOCESE OF OMAHA, Neb., Jan. 13, 1895.

REV. D. A. QUINN:

Rev. Dear Sir—Having heard a good deal spoken of your system of shorthand for the typewriter, please send me the book of instruction and bill of costs.

Yours in Xto,

REV. A. M. CALANERI,

Chancellor.

After the Rev. Chancellor received the book, in less than two weeks he wrote the Author a letter in Stenotypy, which evinced a thorough knowledge of its principles.

COLUMBIA, Mo., Jan. 22, 1895.

REV. D. A. QUINN:

Dear Rev. Sir—I thank you very heartily for your copies of Stenotypy. It is just the needed thing. I handed the second copy to an expert typewriter and stenographer, who declared it GOOD. Accept again my thanks, and best wishes for your continued success.

Yours in Xt,

REV. L. F. O'REILLY.

ST. PAUL'S ACADEMY,

ST. PAUL, Ore., Dec. 27, 1894.

REV. D. A. QUINN:

Dear Rev. Father—The three copies of Stenotypy arrived while I was absent—hence the delay in acknowledging the great favor of which I have been the happy recipient, and which I appreciate more than words can express. The Sister who has undertaken to learn this shorthand typewriting is charmed with its simplicity and the ease in attaining a practical knowledge of this time-saving art. With heartful thanks for your kindness, and wishing you all the joys of this holy season, I am, dear Rev. Father,

Yours in Jesus and Mary,

SISTER M. of Jesus, Sup'r.

In the Providence Visitor of October, 1894, (in the editorial column) it was stated that stenographic experts had examined Father Quinn's system of Stenotypy and found that it possessed the merits claimed for it by the Author.

The following letter, dictated by the Treasurer of the American Writing Machine Co., will show what obstacles the invalid Author of Stenotypy may expect to encounter.

THE CALIGRAPH WRITING MACHINE CO.,

HARTFORD, Conn., Dec. 6, 1893.

REV. D. A. QUINN:

Dear Sir—Your letter of Dec. 5, with enclosures, have been received. It is hardly a matter we can decide in a moment, and we would like to weigh further before taking up your system of Stenotypy. At first thought we are inclined to believe that it would be a damage. We should certainly secure the undying *hostility* of the schools."

Very truly yours,

THE AMERICAN WRITING MACHINE Co.

Dictated by GEORGE W. DICKERMAN, Treasurer.

55